INTERRUPTING TRADITION

LOUVAIN THEOLOGICAL & PASTORAL MONOGRAPHS
—————————— 30 ——————————

INTERRUPTING TRADITION

An Essay on Christian Faith in a Postmodern Context

Lieven Boeve

PEETERS PRESS
LOUVAIN – DUDLEY, MA

Library of Congress Cataloging-in-Publication Data

Boeve, L. (Lieven)
[Onderbroken traditie, English]
Interrupting tradition: an essay on Christian faith in a postmodern context / Lieven
Boeve.
    p. cm. -- (Louvain theological & pastoral monographs; 30)
Translation by Brian Doyle.
Includes bibliographical references.
ISBN 90-429-1282-0
    1. Tradition (Theology) 2. Postmodernism--Religious aspects--Christianity.
3. Christianity and other religions. I. Title. II. Series.

BT90.B69513 2002
230--dc21   2003043303

© 2003, Peeters, Bondgenotenlaan 153, 3000 Leuven, Belgium

ISBN 0-8028-2667-9 (W.B. Eerdmans)
ISBN 90-429-1282-0 (Peeters Leuven)
D. 2003/0602/40

TABLE OF CONTENTS

This manuscript is a reworked translation of Lieven Boeve, *Onderbroken traditie. Heeft het christelijke verhaal nog toekomst?*, Kapellen: Pelckmans, 1999. Translation by Brian Doyle.

PREFACE

In many traditionally Christian European societies, Christian faith no longer enjoys the monopoly it once had in giving meaning to human existence. The processes of secularisation and pluralisation have seriously restricted the all-inclusive importance of the Christian horizon of meaning. Postmodernity's criticism of so-called master narratives have undermined the so-called absolutist and universalist truth claims of religious traditions and modern ideologies. The postmodern context challenges today's theologians, requiring them to engage yet again in theology's age-old project of *fides quaerens intellectum*, 'faith seeking understanding'.

The present essay is an attempt at a cultural-theological reflection upon the challenges emerging from the contemporary context. Departing from a Roman Catholic theological perspective, our aim is to engage in an interdisciplinary dialogue with the results of cultural, sociological and philosophical analysis. The fundamental theological insights undergirding our reflections are mentioned only briefly in the text. I have discussed these at length elsewhere, and detailed references are included in the notes.

This work has come to fruition over quite some time and I am indebted to many colleagues and friends in and outside the academy. First of all I would like to thank my colleagues and research collaborators in the Department of Dogmatic Theology, and the Research Group 'Theology in a Postmodern Context' at the Faculty of Theology, K.U.Leuven. Over the years they have offered me a very inspiring and challenging study and discussion environment, which I abundantly appreciate. I would like to express my debt of gratitude to Brian Doyle, my translator, and to Terrence

Merrigan, editor of LTPM Series who supported the publication of this essay. Grateful acknowledgement is also made to Uitgeverij Pelckmans for the permission to publish this re-edited translation from the Dutch original, and to Peeters Press for this publication. Further, I must also record my thanks to the Flemish Fund for Scientific Research (FWO-V) and the K.U.Leuven Research Fund, which have provided generous financial support for the research projects in which I have been involved in recent years.

Finally, in line with the adage that theology involves biography, I would like to dedicate this work to the ones with whom I am most intimately bound, my wife Maryleen and my three children Maren, Timon and Joren.

INTRODUCTION

Coming to terms with the problem of meaning in today's world is a matter that obliges us to account for the fact that religions and worldviews are characterised by their plurality. It was not so long ago that the Christian faith in the West constituted the virtually unquestioned source in which people sought to find meaning for their everyday practices. In contemporary Western societies, a variety of old and new religions and worldviews have taken their place in the atlas of fundamental life options side by side with the so-called world religions. Complex phenomena such as *New Age* and the proliferation of new religious movements and groups make it all the more difficult to get a grasp of the situation. Even within the major religions there is evidence of a variety of distinct ways of experiencing and perceiving their core features. In addition, clear examples of cross-pollination between religions can be observed whereby specific elements are taken over from one religious and cultural tradition into another. The African Christ takes the form of a tribal elder; the Asian Jesus is presented as a guru. In the West, God is presented at one moment as a father and at another as a liberator, saviour, comforter, friend, partner, mother as well as unnameable spirit, driving force, divine energy, 'higher form'. Not surprisingly, western contemplative spirits are drawn to the mysticism of eastern Buddhism.

1. QUESTIONS AND ANSWERS

For Christians, this externally and internally observed and experienced plurality raises a number of questions that provide substantial food

for thought. Internal plurality raises questions concerning the place
of tradition in the Christian faith as it has taken shape within our
Churches. To what extent does religious expression from the past
determine our present day lived faith? Is this warranted? Is devi-
ation from past and once customary patterns of religious behaviour justifiable and indeed desirable, or should we endeavour to
avoid such evolutions? What legitimates such deviations in the
first place? In this respect, we must deal with the question of the
development of tradition: can a tradition develop? Can it change?
Does such change and development always result in 'more and
better', or do changes in the tradition have further, unseen consequences? Do contemporary Christians live and believe in the same
way as their forefathers and mothers a couple of centuries ago?
What status does the Christian tradition enjoy in our world of
plurality? Are all the traditions to be discerned in our postmodern
era equally true and valid or at least of equal value? Is it possible
for one tradition to claim a degree of privilege over the others
when it comes to the question of truth? Is there a single tradition
that embraces and unifies the truth to be found in all the other traditions?

Such questions would appear to be the specific territory of the
(professional) theologian. It would be impossible, however, to deal
with such questions in isolation from the most significant problem
that faces the Churches in many European countries: can *the
flagging and ineffectual transmission of the Christian tradition*
guarantee the survival of the Christian narrative? For decades,
Christians have found themselves increasingly unable to fruitfully
initiate the following generations into the Christian faith. As such,
the very transmission of the tradition as such is in serious danger.
The still fairly reasonable percentages of people who participate in
the 'rites of passage' (baptism, confirmation, marriage, funeral)
tend to obscure the reality of the situation. Studies have shown that

secularisation is continuing at a faster pace than ever before[1] and not only with respect to people's faith engagement and their Church involvement. Culture itself is undergoing a process of detraditionalisation. Professors of (art) history, for example, complain that their students are becoming less and less familiar with the classics of 'Christian culture' as the years go by. Their teaching in this regard, they lament, is obliged to limit itself to the very minimum of introductory information, and can no longer delve into the abundant riches of Christianity's aesthetical history.

For some, this painful situation is to be blamed on the lamentable and unattractive state in which the faith is and continues to be presented to our contemporaries. They insist that there is an urgent need to seek out a new and attractive language that is both

---

[1] See K. Dobbelaere, M. Elchardus, et al., *Verloren zekerheid. De Belgen en hun waarden, overtuigingen en houdingen* (Tielt, 2000). This volume is the result of the third European Value Study. The titles of the three subsequent books reporting these results are particularly telling. In 1984 the research group in charge of the study published *The Silent Turn*, a report that made it evident that Belgium had turned away from a more traditional Roman Catholic profile: ed. J. Kerkhofs & R. Rezsohazy, *De stille ommekeer: oude en nieuwe waarden in het België van de jaren tachtig* (Tielt, 1984). In 1992 the same group published *The Accelerated Turn*, claiming that changes were evolving faster than ever: *De versnelde ommekeer* (Tielt, 1992). The title of the third book, *Lost Certainty* (2000), indicates that the processes of detraditionalisation are reaching their end. In no more than a few decades, Belgium has turned from a society perceived as more or less Catholic into a secularised and pluralized country. Some of the research results illustrate this situation well. When Belgians were asked to define themselves in terms of religious affiliation, 47,4% described themselves as Catholic, 1,2% as Protestant and 15,3% claimed to be Christian without being Protestant or Catholic (p. 119). In 1967 52% of the Flemish people (for Belgium as a whole 42,9%) attended Sunday services on a weekly basis, in 1998 this was reduced to 12,7% (Belgium 11,2%) (p. 123). In 1967 96,1% of newborn children were baptised in Flanders, in 1998 73%. The Belgian figures for 1998 fell by a further 8% (64,7). Marrying in the church (as opposed to an exclusively civil marriage): for Flanders 91,8% in 1967, 51,2% in 1998; for Belgium 86,1% in 1967, 49,2% in 1998 (p. 123).

plausible and convincing. For others, this is not enough. They maintain that not only the language is in need of thorough reorganisation but also the tradition itself. In their view, it is precisely because the actual form the tradition tends to take (*in casu*, at least for the most part, the Church) is so out of touch with modern culture and society that the Church is obstructed in its efforts to initiate. Only when the Church is able to bring its doctrine, ethics, spirituality and organisational structures up to date will faith become a credible option once again. Others still exploit their awareness of the gulf between faith and culture to argue the contrary position: it is culture that has alienated itself from the faith. In their eyes, only the restoration of tradition as tradition and not its assimilation to culture can save the Christian faith from final obliteration. Those who adapt and assimilate are already responsible for the evaporation of the Christian faith into the culture that surrounds it.

Whatever the proposed remedy, the *diagnosis* leads one to the unavoidable conclusion that *an ever-increasing gulf exists between contemporary culture and the Christian faith*. The days of 'traditional', cultural Christianity are numbered. Even committed Christians are finding it difficult to maintain their faith convictions in the face of such ongoing discrepancies. Is faith in today's world still a reasonable option? Is it still possible to justify such faith at a time when belief in God has become overshadowed and socially implausible? Even where many continue to cultivate (often only vague) religious sentiments, the Christian faith continues to be seen as out of date, naive, and even dangerous. Our culture no longer supports the notion of faith in God. For some, moreover, the very fact that the Church once enjoyed a quasi-monopoly with respect to people's fundamental life options has led to a considerable degree of negative prejudice, which ultimately stands in the way of demonstrating the actual plausibility of the Christian faith.

2. GOALS AND PRIORITIES

From the perspective of the transmission of the Christian tradition — the 'tradition' in its active sense — the present study will endeavour to answer the questions formulated in the preceding paragraph. To what extent can the Christian faith still offer meaning to contemporary men and women and the communities to which they belong? It is our conviction that every new context challenges the Christian tradition to reformulate its offer of meaning in a credible manner. This reformulation has happened countless times in the past and must also happen today if the Christian faith still hopes to survive into the 22nd century. This implies, in the first place, that traditionalism, the withdrawal into one's own sense of absolute right, has few guarantees if any to offer in this process of survival. At the same time, however, far-reaching adaptation to the postmodern context is also unjustified. Only a new dialogue between tradition and context, with due respect for (and indeed thanks to) the expanding gulf between both, can offer any kind of future.

The goal of the present monograph is to present the process and results of our attempted dialogue in three parts. Part one will endeavour to clarify the situation in which the Christian tradition finds itself today. To this end, the first chapter will offer a sketch of the tradition as such and how it developed. At this stage we will introduce one of the core concepts of our argument: 'recontextualisation'. Tradition develops when the context shifts. In chapter two we will offer a more in-depth analysis of the radical confrontation between the Christian faith and modernity. The modern processes of change and the intellectual currents that accompanied them did not tend as much to challenge the Christian tradition to develop but rather to put it radically to the test. The Church reacted in a variety of ways to this challenge: from defensive retrenchment to progressive adaptation. In chapter three we will follow this historical line of thought through to the present day and offer an analysis of the problem of fundamental life options in what is now referred to as the postmodern context. Indeed, for a number of decades our context has been characterised by an ideological plurality that has placed the formation of human identity in a new perspective. Identity formation has become less and less a matter of custom and more and more a matter of choice. The cultural Christianity which was able to survive in modernity would appear to have been replaced in postmodernity by a volunteer Church, a church which seeks to follow a middle path between the extremes of relativism and fundamentalism.

Having thus presented the perspective of our study we are confronted by the primary question to which it gives rise: how can the Christian faith recontextualise itself in a credible manner in a context that is characterised by radical plurality? Are there points of contact with the actual context that might help this process along? In what way must the process of recontextualisation, the renewed dynamic interaction of tradition and context, ultimately take place? In part two of our study we will offer an analysis of the critical consciousness that has emerged in our postmodern context. The nature of our interaction with plurality and difference is of crucial importance in this regard. In chapter four we offer a sketch of the strategies that tend to determine this interaction together with a discussion of the 'master narratives' of 'denial' and 'disempowerment'. In chapter five we will unfold a positive example of contextual critical consciousness, resulting in the model of the 'open narrative', a narrative type which, in contrast to the 'master narrative' structure, has the capacity to take on the challenge of, and confrontation with, plurality and difference with both determination and respect. In chapter six our investigation will try to determine whether this model of contextual critical consciousness can play an identifiable role in the Christian faith: is a Christian *open* narrative possible?

In part three of our study we will attempt to bring the process of recontextualisation to completion. It is clearly insufficient to simply state that the Christian narrative has the capacity to transform itself into an open narrative. Genuine recontextualisation calls for a positive response to a second and more fundamental question: are there theological grounds upon which the Christian narrative can be spoken of as an open narrative? Is an open *Christian* narrative possible and, if so, what are the consequences thereof? In the seventh chapter we will endeavour to answer these questions on the basis of a study of the foundations of the Christian narrative: faith in Jesus Christ. We will present an image of Jesus that not only legitimates our theological recontextualisation of the Christian narrative as an open narrative but also provides it with appropriate expression. We will take this line of thought a step further in chapter eight in which contextual and credible speaking and thinking about God has pride of place. In this regard, the rediscovery of the tradition of negative theology provides a source of inspiration with its reference to God as the unthinkable, as the boundary of all thinking and speaking. Rooted in a context of religious plurality, chapter nine will endeavour to determine the extent to which the claims of the Christian faith can still be substantiated. What is the status of Christianity in comparison with and in relation to the other world religions? In other words, how should we understand the concept of religious truth?

By way of conclusion we will briefly outline the position of the Christian individual today, employing six distinct points of accent.

3. GETTING STARTED

In his book *Cultuur, religie, geloof?*,[2] Antoon Vergote distinguishes the following shared religious characteristics: myths, prayers (of

---

[2] A. Vergote, *Cultuur, religie en geloof* (Leuven, 1989) 50ff. See also the first chapter of his *Modernité et christianisme: interrogations critiques réciproques* (Paris, 1999).

petition, praise, thanksgiving, guilt and reconciliation), rites, symbolic presentations of the divinity,[3] ethics[4] and religious experience. The interplay between these diverse aspects, which cannot in fact be considered in isolation from one another, reveals that *religion* has a *total and all-inclusive character* that determines every aspect of human life. Just as a person finds him/herself situated in a given 'language' so the religious person/community finds him/her/itself situated in a given religion that can never as such be constructed. In the same manner as the 'family' in which each of us is situated, so religion structures the relational field of religious individuals and communities.[5]

In its own way, Christianity reflects the family characteristics of religion as summarised by Vergote. Vergote, however, objects to an unnuanced characterisation of Christianity as 'cultural religion'. The God of Christianity is regarded as totally Other with respect to the world (creator and creation are radically distinguished). This leads to a radical de-mythologisation of the Christian faith and a radical departure from the profile of the cultural religion. The structure of the Christian religion as such does not (should not) permit religion and culture to be understood as two sides of the same coin. Rooted in a strictly-maintained distinction between God (as the Other), on the one hand, and the human person, the world, nature

---

[3] Not infrequently elements taken from the natural or social environment were considered to embody the divine and as such often became the subject of divine adoration (e.g., the cult of the bull or of the sun).

[4] 'Ethics' is understood here in the broadest sense of the term as a set of religiously motivated guidelines intended to regulate individual and social existence, whereby the distinction between ritual and ethical prescriptions is seldom made.

[5] Vergote notes that it is not accidental that such family-oriented structures tend to emerge at the core of many religions, that the Divinity or religious leaders are often referred to as mother or father, that individuals are addressed as brother or sister and that communities tend to be styled sisterhoods or brotherhoods.

and culture, on the other, the latter are deprived of divinity (the sun and the king, for example, are no longer considered to be divine). While elements of culture have the capacity to refer beyond the earthly to the Other, they no longer represent the divine in any substantial way. Religion becomes faith. It no longer presumes itself to be taken up in an all-inclusive religious reality in which the divine is fully present and within which human persons and communities play an unavoidable role. Religion is transformed into a personally and communally experienced and expressed faith, oriented towards a personal God experienced and identified as love.[6]

This implies that the disappearance of a particular culture does not prevent the Christian religion from continuing in a different culture and inculturating itself therein.[7] What Vergote ascribes to Christianity at the structural level, namely, that it is by its very nature a 'religion of faith', and not a cultural religion, only became manifest as such in the modern period. Indeed, from the sixteenth century onwards, Christian faith and modern culture definitively went their separate ways. From the cultural perspective, Christian faith was considered less and less plausible as it increasingly demanded 'a leap of faith', a genuine, conscious option.[8] In the

---

[6] "Believing in the specific sense of the term has to do with the personal assent of a man or woman who freely engages him/herself in support of his/her conviction and who implies by his/her assent that he/she is conscious of being subject to the claim of a message that leaves room for a non-believing response. [...] Cultural religions do not offer an option in this regard because [...] the individual in question is caught up in a religious network from which he/she is unable to withdraw" (*Ibid.*, p. 72).

[7] A further consequence of this shift from cultural religion to faith religion lies in the fact that culture and religion as such are no longer seamlessly conjoined. This, among other things, is one of the preconditions for a religiously motivated critique of culture.

[8] This evolution was 'deferred' in Flanders — and thus provided with a response — by the development of a Christian sub-culture — sometimes referred to as 'pillarisation' — that embraced the lives of its participants in an inclusive

premodern period, and where Christianity enjoyed an undisputed majority status, the Christian faith was firmly embedded in Christian cultures and, in spite of efforts to maintain the distinction between the creator and the created, society and nature were closely linked with the religious and the divine. Life, work, planning and government ultimately served to honour and glorify the Christian God. Change only took place in the modern period when the Christian faith came to be challenged by a culture that had cast off its religious entanglements.

In its own way, the present study seeks to discover the historical and structural dynamics behind the transformation of the Christian religion into a religion of faith, a transformation that has continued through the past centuries and become a fact of life in the last decades.[9]

way (see further chapter 2). It is for this reason that one is often left with the erroneous impression that the evolving separation between faith and culture in many parts of Western Europe only emerged in earnest in the last decades of the 20th century.

  [9] For this last statement, see note 8.

PART 1

CHRISTIAN TRADITION UNDER PRESSURE

———

Recently, while having coffee after lunch, a young priest mentioned that parents often ask him to baptise their newborn child. Rather than approaching their own parish priest (if they have one), they prefer him (someone from their own circle of friends) to baptise their child. Usually the couple in question will already have been alienated to some degree from the local church community for a considerable time and they will often exhibit a lack of familiarity with the Christian faith. This remains true, he insisted, even when such individuals, together with most young people in Flanders, probably took part in their younger years in honouring the highlights of church life and more than likely enjoyed twelve or more years of Christian religious education at school. Nonetheless, one of the parent couples wanted to make the baptism of their child something special, said the young priest. They proposed having their child baptised in the bathroom of their home. In this way, they argued, the baby would really be coming 'home'. Another parent couple, reported a second companion, took part together with their infant son in a communal baptism ceremony in their parish church, but considered that this alone was not enough. Afterwards, all three of them — father, mother and child — went to a sauna. For them, the welcoming of the newcomer could only be fully realised in this way.

I. TRADITION AND ITS DEVELOPMENT

In this first chapter we will briefly examine the phenomenon of Christian tradition together with a number of ways to conceptualise its development. In chapters two and three we will discuss the confrontation between Christian 'tradition-awareness' and modernity and postmodernity respectively.

1. TRADITION

It is virtually impossible in a Western-European context to conceive of the notion 'tradition' without involving Christianity in one form or another. Whether we want to or not, our perspective is unavoidably coloured by our historical context. Every statement we make about tradition betrays our familiarity with the Christian tradition or lack thereof, together with our understanding of the said tradition and our attitude towards it. It is for this reason that theologians, when they endeavour to describe the concept in 'more general, pre-theological terms', unavoidably reveal their own particular perspective with respect to the Christian tradition. This is also true for the definition of K. Rahner and H. Vorgrimler: "Tradition is [...] the transmission, the customary, i.e. the totality of processes and organisations whereby acquired insights, capacities and institutions are passed on from generation to generation. As such it also constitutes the totality of that which is transmitted."[1]

[1] K. Rahner & H. Vorgrimler, *Kleines theologisches Wörterbuch* (Freiburg, 1961) 360.

Tradition is thus, in the first place, the content of transmission, the body of knowledge, narratives, practices, customs, institutions and organisations of a particular community. This community is thus given form and identity by the tradition it maintains. 'To be part of a tradition' means to possess an experiential familiarity with the content thereof, a familiarity which provides one's concrete day to day existence with structure and perspective. The 'transmission of tradition' implies the passing on of a particular way of looking, judging, experiencing, expecting, acting, organising and existing in a society determined by a historically-evolved totality of concrete narratives and customs. When, for example, it is affirmed that Catholic Christians are located within a particular tradition, reference is ultimately being made to the following elements: the seven sacraments, ethical sensitivities and practices (love of one's neighbour and one's enemy, respect for life), Christian teachings and basic Christian metaphors (conversion, discipleship, 'suffering-death-resurrection') that are contained in Scripture and doctrine, Church as community and organisation and so forth.

Tradition, however, also enjoys an *active* significance, pertaining to the actual *handing on of these elements*. As bearer of the tradition, the community endeavours to ensure the continuity of the process of transmission. This process is given form in our day to day existence. The tradition is continually re-confirmed by life itself, by the way we live, by the choices we make, by our perspective on life. Significant elements include: the initiation of new members, the remembrance of what has come down to us from the past in narratives, feasts and rituals, and, no less significant, the confrontation with newness and otherness. Time and again our identity is affirmed anew. Within the Catholic Church, the Church community and in particular its teaching authority presents itself not only as the explicit bearer of the tradition but also as its guardian. Unique moments in which the tradition is transmitted include the Councils and episcopal synods as well as the statements and writings of the popes and the bishops. The transmission of the tradition cannot, however, be limited to such moments. It is something that takes place every day, something woven into the fabric of the concrete lives of communities and the individuals that constitute them.

2. TRADITION AND CHRISTIANITY

In the history of the Church, Christian authors of the second and third centuries such as Irenaeus of Lyon († ca. 200) and Tertullian († ca. 225) were among the first to appeal to the 'tradition'. In their efforts to protect the Christian faith against heretical teachings, they appealed to the reliability of the *apostolic tradition*, the indisputable truth of which they ascribed to the unbroken chain of bishops in the various churches from the time of the apostles. The authenticity of the truth was thus considered to be rooted in its origins. At the same time, tradition and ordained ministry (apostolic succession) were also considered to have been conjoined from the outset.

In contrast to the rather broad definition of tradition described above, it is striking that tradition in the Christian context came to exhibit a somewhat *doctrinal character* from the first centuries onwards. Tradition came to serve primarily as an argument in the determination of *orthodoxy* ('correct teaching'). For Vincent of Lérins (†450), for example, a true doctrinal teaching or true 'dogma' was and continued to be maintained always (*semper*), everywhere (*ubique*) and by everyone (*ab omnibus*). Actual consensus was considered insufficient if it did not include previous generations of Christians dating back to the beginning of Christianity.[2]

---

[2] "In ipsa item catholica ecclesia magnopere curandum est, ut id teneamus, quod ubique, quod semper, quod ab omnibus creditum est; hoc est etenim vere proprieque catholicum", Vincent of Lérins, *Commonitorium* II (3) (= *Commonitorium pro*

The *Church Fathers* (the most prominent bishops of Christian antiquity) not only used the tradition in their arguments, they also and to a significant degree gave shape to what we now refer to as the Christian tradition. Countering both pagan philosophical theories and religions, they spared nothing in their efforts to explain and defend the truth of Christianity. In this regard they made an initial distinction between apostolic writings and non-apostolic writings (apocrypha), thereby determining the canon of the New Testament. Only the Gospels, the Acts of the Apostles, the Epistles and the Apocalypse, which had found general acceptance in the liturgy and had thus been tested for their orthodoxy, were recognised as the source and norm of authentic faith. During various Synods and Councils, the Church Fathers also formulated 'symbola', confessions of faith. They thus attempted to establish correct teaching concerning, among other things, the Trinity (one God in three persons, Father, Son and Holy Spirit) and the person of Jesus Christ (both God and human).[3] Against the background of the Hellenistic culture of late antiquity, they also set about the reflexive unfolding of the Christian faith and established what we now refer to as theology. As the result of a dialogue between faith and ancient philosophical reflection they developed a contextually-embedded understanding of faith. Christianity's claim to truth was also at stake here. Augustine (†430), bishop of Hippo in North Africa, for example, considered the Christian faith to be the true philosophy, greater than any other doctrine.[4]

catholicae fidei antiquitate et universitate adversus profanas omnium haereticorum novitates [ed. D.A. Jülicher], Sammlung ausgewählter kirchen- und dogmengeschichtlichen Quellenschriften, 10 (Freiburg/Leipzig, 1895, ²1925).

  [3] The councils of Nicea (325) and Constantinople (381) respectively dealt with the divinity of the Son and the Spirit; the council of Chalcedon (451) professed the christological doctrine of the two natures in one person.

  [4] It is worthy of note in regard to this latter development that *tradition* and *theology* have a mutually constitutive yet paradoxical relationship with respect to

The Christian tradition and its use as argument took form within a highly specific historical context. Although this led, as we have noted, to a focus on the doctrinal dimension of the concept of tradition in the early Church, one would be wrong to assume that such a doctrinal elaboration took place in isolation *from authentic religious life* or spiritual dedication to the God of Jesus Christ within a broader ecclesial framework. The opposite in fact is closer to the truth. Indeed, doctrinal development was ultimately intended to protect this broader framework. The tone, however, had been set and the doctrinal dimension became more and more important as history unfolded. In the context of Catholic theology, tradition came to be identified to a large degree with the content and process of the transmission of Christian truth. This truth is revealed in the Scriptures and it 'further unfolds' and comes to completion in the life of the Church 'under the guidance of the Holy Spirit'.[5] This conviction is clearly confirmed in the Church's controversies with the Reformation. Against Luther's 'sola scriptura' principle, which accepted only the Scriptures as the source of revealed truth, the Council of Trent (1545-63) insisted that both the Scriptures and the oral tradition together constituted the actual source thereof.[6] The Second Vatican Council (1962-65) upheld this conviction although it drew attention to the close relationship between the two.

one another. Theology depends on tradition for its origins while the theologian (for whom the tradition constitutes the object of his/her research) simultaneously contributes to the construction of the self-same tradition.

[5] Rahner & Vorgrimler, *Kleines theologisches Wörterbuch*, 361.

[6] From the first decree of the fourth Session of the Council of Trent (April, 8, 1546), *On the Acceptance of the Sacred Books and Apostolic Traditions*: "The council clearly perceives that this truth [of salvation] and rule [of conduct] are contained in written books and in unwritten traditions which were received by the apostles from the mouth of Christ himself, or else have come down to us, handed on as it were from the apostles themselves at the inspiration of the Holy Spirit" (ed. N.P. Tanner, *Decrees of the Ecumenical Councils*, London/Washington, DC, 1990, vol. 2, p. 663).

Moreover, Vatican II also insisted on the dynamic and embedded character of revealed truth, which the Church passed on from generation to generation in its teaching, life and cult. The doctrinal tone of the Catholic understanding of tradition was thus further nuanced and its broader scope reaffirmed.[7]

A more contemporary theological definition of 'tradition' might run as follows: "The term tradition refers to the subject, the process, and the content of the transmission of faith through which the identity, the continuity, and the productive unfolding of the message of revelation in the community of faith is made possible."[8] In other words, tradition stands for the 'that' and the 'what' of the mediation of the faith. Furthermore, such a definition shows that not only is tradition the precondition which makes the identity, continuity and unfolding of the message of revelation in the faith community possible, but that it also constitutes the precondition for making the faith community itself possible in as far as it makes faith possible. There is no Christian faith or Christian community outside the framework of the Christian tradition.

3. THE DEVELOPMENT OF TRADITION

Cumulative models

The increasing modern awareness that truth has a history[9] led theologians from (at least) the nineteenth century onwards to reflect on the idea of the development of tradition. The understanding that

---

[7] See the Dogmatic Constitution on Divine Revelation *Dei verbum* (November 18, 1965), in Tanner, *Decrees,* 971-981.

[8] W. Beinert, "Tradition," ed. W. Beinert & F.S. Fiorenza, *Handbook of Catholic Theology* (New York, 1995) 712-716, p. 712.

[9] Developments in the world of science — which led, among other things, to Darwin's evolutionism — and in philosophy gave rise to the insight that history implied development, or at the very least, change.

such development was simply the unfolding of the truth which was already present in revelation (Scriptures), was particularly in vogue. The development of tradition was seen as cumulative, as the elucidation and explication of what was already implicitly known. Confrontations with newness and otherness were considered in this regard to be situations that stimulated further unfolding of the tradition, in some instances even making it necessary. Examples here include the various heresies and non-Christian teachings that obliged the Church Fathers to seek further clarification, the Orthodox and Protestant schisms, and conflicts with the emerging natural sciences and social ideologies of the modern period. Such conflicts made it necessary to express the implicitly available and accepted truth in explicit dogmatic formulas under the teaching authority of the pope and the Councils. Understood in this way, the development of tradition can already be seen to exhibit, albeit in a hidden way, an early interest in the historicity and context-relatedness of the Christian faith. Nevertheless, the relationship between history and context, on the one hand, and tradition, on the other, remained external and extrinsic. New events and conflicts were merely the occasion of potential development, they were not understood to have made an essential contribution to the content of the tradition itself. The truth in fact was already available and only had to be unearthed and unravelled.[10]

Recontextualisation: the tradition shifts when the context changes

After the Second Vatican Council (1963-65) the perspective changed. Theologians such as Edward Schillebeeckx and Hans Küng drew

---

[10] Such an understanding of tradition also lies behind the medieval distinction between *Traditio* and *traditiones*: *Traditio* stands hereby for the substance of the Christian truth as proclaimed by the Church throughout the centuries while *traditiones* stand for the particular articulations of this truth adapted to time and place. See Y. Congar, *La Tradition et les traditions*, 2 vols. (Paris, 1960-1963).

increasing attention to the *contextual* character of tradition and the development thereof.[11] From the historical perspective, political, social and cultural circumstances and modes of thought were understood to have had a profound influence on the development of tradition. For the aforementioned theologians, the idea of a 'Christian Tradition' that had survived unchanged (or 'changed' only in the cumulative sense) down through the centuries was untenable.

In principle, every tradition is inseparably *embedded in a specific historical context* that has made an essential contribution to the form thereof. The formulation of Jesus Christ's simultaneous humanity and divinity at Chalcedon (451), for example, simply cannot be understood if one does not pay sufficient attention to the contemporary context and the modes of thought which were present and functioned therein. While it goes without saying that this does not mean that the Christian faith can be reduced to the context and its modes of thought, it does tend to imply that the uniqueness of the Christian faith ultimately took shape in relationship to and by use of the context. It follows, therefore, that every shift in context constitutes a challenge to the Christian tradition to reformulate itself in dialogue with the relevant context. With every shift in context the existing shape of the tradition will lose a degree of plausibility and accessibility. Such *recontextualisation* of the tradition is simultaneously tied up with the actual life of faith, with concrete faith experiences, on the one hand, and the transmitted tradition, on the other. New and contextually available modes of thought, narrative material and ways of doing things are taken on board and contribute to a contextual explication of what one experiences as Christian identity. As further shifts in the context take

[11] See E. Schillebeeckx, *Mensen als verhaal van God* (Baarn, 1989) (E.T.: *Church: The Human Story of God*, transl. J. Bowden (London, 1990)); H. Küng, *Theologie im Aufbruch. Eine ökumenische Grundlegung* (Munich, 1987).

place, this specific actualisation of the tradition is challenged in turn to face the question of further recontextualisation. Anselm of Canterbury (†1109), for example, made use of German legal doctrine to explain the significance of Jesus' death on the cross. Jesus saved us on the cross because he offered recompense for our sins. By analogy with the way a feudal lord demands recompense from his disloyal and unfaithful subjects, so Jesus, by his death on the cross, restored God's honour which had been wounded by sin. Given the evolution in our sense of justice through the centuries, however, Anselm's doctrine of atonement comes across in our age as somewhat strange, doing violence, among other things, to the way in which Christians today speak of a loving God. Nevertheless, in Anselm's world this theological declaration was quite acceptable: it expressed people's existentially-felt consciousness of guilt and powerlessness before God, and how Christ was able to free them from this, in a contextually plausible and insightful way.[12]

The result of recontextualisation is thus *not so much 'more' tradition but rather 'different' tradition.* Under the influence of the context, our way of looking at things, the very paradigm with which we experience and conceptualise faith and tradition, is changed. When compared with the situation in the fourth century, for example, our present experience of faith and reflection thereon is unmistakably coloured by the influence of Germanic culture that has its roots in the fourth and fifth century invasions of the Roman Empire. The same can be said of the emergence of the natural sciences from the fifteenth century onwards, and the emancipatory impulses which irretrievably altered the complexion of our day-to-day environment in the eighteenth and nineteenth centuries. In our contemporary circumstances, the growing awareness of plurality in our experience of reality is a primary determinative factor, calling into

[12] For further details, see Chapter 7, first section.

question the traditional truth claims of the Christian faith. We shall return to these questions in the following chapters.

A non-cumulative, dynamic perspective on the development of tradition, such as recontextualisation, implies that we are not simply receivers of the tradition that comes to us from the past. We are *not only heirs to the inheritance, we are also its testators.* Living tradition is also our responsibility. By way of recontextualisation, we are called to experience and reflect upon Christianity's offer of meaning and to pass it on. This certainly does not mean that the tradition simply adapts itself — some will say 'surrenders' itself — to time and context. What it does imply is that every time and context challenges us to give shape to the message of God's love revealed in Jesus Christ in a contemporary way. If we do not accept this challenge we run the risk of sliding into inauthenticity.

The Christian narrative no longer exists, we only have access to it through its relation to the context. In the establishment of the canon of the new Testament, the early Church selected writings that have remained normative for the Christian faith. It is in this way that the same early Church instigated a process of interpretation and transmission that remains in effect to the present day. From the perspective of history, the Christian narrative worked its way through a variety of successive contexts, continually recontextualising along the way. As a result it took on a multitude of different forms that were not always reconcilable with those it had left behind.

Theology and recontextualisation

What is true for the Christian tradition in general is also true for the development of theology. Theology stands for the reflexive (i.e., at the conceptual level) expression of the sense of faith as it is lived in the faith community of which the theologian is a part. Theology is the result of what Anselm of Canterbury described as *fides quaerens intellectum*: 'faith seeking understanding' or, better still, 'the one who participates in reality as a believer wants to make his or her faith a source of insight in order to arrive at a Christian understanding of reality'. In a systematic and plausible manner, the theologian endeavours to put the life of faith into words and to express his or her participation as a Christian believer in reality. The credibility of theology is dependent on its embeddedness in the temporal and spatial context. Plausibility is always contextual plausibility: any effectively-acquired theological insight will always be conditioned by and measured against the criteria in vogue in the context. Under the influence of the natural sciences, the person who reflects today on God as creator will be unlikely to simply locate the divine act of creation at the beginning of the history of physical evolution — (prior to) the big bang. Indeed, he or she will be more likely to refer to the fundamental distinction between the scientific discourse and the believer's faith claims.

In terms of methodology, theology has always stood in relation to the philosophy (and more recently the humanities and [social] sciences) which dominated the context, frequently borrowing its models, patterns, ideas and terminology in order to develop, structure, motivate and ornament its own explanations. Philosophy in turn was most often a clarification of a broader contextual understanding of life. This implied that the theologian who shared this understanding was probably more likely to sense some degree of alliance with (one of) the positions developed by the said philosophical context. By borrowing models or other elements from the philosophical context, the theologian was then able to evoke truths of faith in a new, refreshing and contextually-integrated manner. Of course the theologian did not then become a philosopher among philosophers (or social scientist among social scientists). Rather, he or she employed philosophy in the best tradition of the 'philosophia ancilla theologiae' (philosophy as the handmaid of theology) in the drafting of his or her own theological narrative. In short: in the encounter with philosophy and the selective integration of promising models for constructing its own rationality, theology recontextualised itself. More often than not, this process went hand in hand with controversy, especially since the new contextually relevant models — which enjoyed a greater capacity to give contextual plausibility to the experience of faith — tended to nudge the older models out of the way.

Theology only exists, therefore, as contextual theology, and the development of tradition only as an ongoing process of recontextualisation. It is for this reason that 'contextual theology' is not only the business of missiologists or sub-culture and third-world theologians.[13] Rather, it is inalienably at work in every legitimate theology. The present-day demand for a theological recontextualisation of the Christian tradition in diverse (non-European[14]) cultural contexts is only a synchronic realisation of a diachronic process that has been at work for centuries. Moreover, evident shifts in the European context seem to suggest that European theology is, more than ever before, itself in need of recontextualisation.

4. SOME EXAMPLES

The Old Testament: from Judaeo-Aramaic to Judaeo-Hellenistic context

At a workshop on the challenge of cultural (and thus contextual) newness for theology, the Old Testament exegete Jacques Vermeylen tried to show that the question of culture in the theological

---

[13] See, for example, P. Beer, *Kontextuelle Theologie. Überlegungen zu ihrer systematischen Grundlegung* (Paderborn, 1995).

[14] V. Neckebrouck, *La tierce Église devant le problème de la culture,* Neue Zeitschrift für Missionswissenschaft. Supplementa, 36 (Immensee, 1987).

endeavour is an ongoing one related to every time and place.[15] In defence of his proposition — basically the same as we have been suggesting so far: when the context changes theology recontextualises — he focused his attention on the reception of Hellenistic culture in a number of the younger books of the Old Testament in which a variety of different attitudes can be discerned with respect to the rich Hellenistic culture which was confronting Judaism at the time. These include: 'assimilation', 'prejudice in the name of traditional values', 'making distinctions and expressing them'.

While Qoheleth may have assimilated Hellenism, this is certainly not the case with Jesus Sirach: Greek culture is dangerous and to be rejected — only the strict maintenance of the Law offers any future. The book of Daniel also shares this critical stance but is more radical: Hellenism is the incarnation of Evil itself. A product of the Jewish community of Alexandria, the book of Wisdom, on the other hand, is the example par excellence of the integration of Jewish faith and Hellenistic culture: Greek culture is employed as an instrument in the service of faith in YHWH. Vermeylen raises a number of considerations in this regard. In the first instance, these texts constitute a witness to the internal plurality of responses within Judaism to the challenge formed by Hellenism. The fact that they were (in part) canonised officially sanctions this plurality. Nevertheless, the New Testament and patristic writings reveal that the various responses are not of equal value. Indeed, the option of the young Church was analogous to that of the book of Wisdom: with the decision to send out missionaries among the pagans, Greek culture was gratefully employed in the defence of the faith. Ultimately, this choice of Greek culture became so deeply rooted in the

---

[15] Louvain-la-Neuve, January 28-29, 1994. Published as J. Vermeylen, "Foi traditionnelle et culture nouvelle: un précédent biblique," ed. Id., *Cultures et théologies en Europe. Jalons pour un dialogue,* Association européenne de théologie catholique, section belge francophone (Paris, 1995) 13-42.

Christian tradition that many, even up to the present day, consider it to be irreplaceably and inseparably bound up with the Christian faith. The underlying metaphysics and anthropology of Hellenistic culture, however, are no longer those of today. Vermeylen concluded, therefore, with a question: "Can Christianity be faithfully expressed in categories which are no longer borrowed from inherited Greek concepts but which introduce a multiplicity of contemporary cultural sensitivities?" For Vermeylen the answer to this question had to be 'Yes'.[16]

The theological project of Thomas Aquinas

The history of theology teaches us that Christian faith has also been subjected to many and profound challenges by Greek thought.[17] The context of the first Christians — and certainly the elite among them — was largely conditioned by this thought, especially by Platonism.[18] To a significant extent, Greek thought determined the approach of first-century Christians reflecting on their faith and attempting to defend its rationality. It should not come as a surprise, therefore, that this philosophical-conceptual *instrumentarium,* which determined early Christian modes of thought, was adopted and in this process of adoption transformed: in other words, it was recontextualised. The contribution of Greek philosophy to the

[16] *Ibid.*, p. 42

[17] See, among others, A. Peperzak, *Tussen filosofie en theologie* (Kampen/ Kapellen, 1991); J.A. Bonsor, *Athens and Jerusalem. The Role of Philosophy in Theology* (Mahwah, 1993).

[18] See, among others, C. Stead, *Philosophie und Theologie. I. Die Zeit der Alten Kirche,* Kohlhammer Theologische Wissenschaft, 14.4 (Stuttgart, 1990) 47. Stead argues that Epicurism was on the wane while Stoicism was only active in the moral philosophical arena. The Pythagoreans had associated themselves for the most part with Platonism while Aristotelianism could claim few if any eminent representatives. A revival of Scepticism offered some degree of reaction. In the meantime, Platonism as such had assimilated a number of Pythagorean and Stoic elements.

emerging theological endeavour cannot easily be disclaimed.[19] Theologians, however, did not simply adopt elements of Greek thought as if they somehow fulfilled a need to supplement an already existing narrative. Rather — and here our search extends to the very origins of theology[20] — Greek thought determined the way in which Christians expressed themselves reflexively. As such, theology as reflection found its ally in Greek thought.[21]

One of the better examples of the way in which philosophy — and its successful endeavour to reflexively clarify the context — provided theology with models for expressing its own rationality, can be found in the assimilation of Aristotle's philosophy by Thomas Aquinas (1225-74). From roughly the middle of the twelfth century onwards, the context in which theology was done underwent drastic changes. While theology up until then had become the more or less exclusive domain of the monastic orders, university theology faculties now began to emerge in the cities, structured along the lines of the city guilds. From this point onwards, the theology faculties largely took over theology as an academic pursuit. At the same time — mostly under the influence of Islamic thinkers — the rediscovered works of Aristotle increasingly gained importance in intellectual life. In 1255, for example, the then known

---

[19] *Ibid.*, p. 57: "Philosophy's contribution to early Christian thought is virtually beyond dispute. In spite of frequent disagreements concerning the evaluation thereof it remains an established fact." The author elaborates this statement further, including reflection concerning the presentation and description of God, the use of the words 'substance', 'person', 'logos' and 'equal in essence' and the problems concerning the two natures in Christ.

[20] See D. Allen, *Philosophy for Understanding Theology* (Atlanta, 1985) 5: "We would not have the discipline of theology without the Hellenic attitude in Christians that leads them to press questions about the Bible and the relations of the bible to other knowledge."

[21] See in this regard the inspiration that Augustine found in the neo-Platonism of Plotinus.

works of Aristotle were introduced as obligatory reading for the students of the faculty of arts at the university of Paris. Given the fact that those who attended university were obliged to follow the programme of this faculty as part of their basic training, the intellectual climate came to be increasingly determined by this mode of thinking.

These changes in context had far-reaching consequences for the practice of theology. While theology at that moment tended to be heavily influenced by Platonic thought, an autonomous philosophy was developing in the faculty of arts based on the study of Aristotle. Theology was thus being confronted with a new situation to which, given its shape at the time, it did not have a ready response beyond that of rejection. The challenge, however, had been made: how could theology deal with an autonomous human mode of thought that could apparently be acquired without divine assistance or grace? "The endeavour to link human knowledge with Christian revelation took on a different character when Aristotle and no longer Plato became representative for human potential and capacity. Time and again the boundaries between nature and grace, faith and reason, philosophy and theology were redrawn."[22] The study of Aristotle provided models and a vocabulary for recontextualising theology.[23] Such a recontextualisation was necessary because Aristotelianism had come to dominate and determine the intellectual climate. The form in which theology had been cast up to that point was no longer capable of rendering the reflexive unfolding of

---

[22] D. Allen, *Philosophy for Understanding Theology*, 109. (See the section: "Aristotle and the Creation of Scholastic Theology," 107-136).

[23] See, among others, J. Decorte, *Waarheid als weg. Beknopte geschiedenis van de middeleeuwse wijsbegeerte* (Kapellen/Kampen, 1992) 176: Thomas considers Aristotelianism to possess "many interesting conceptual building blocks that have the capacity to significantly facilitate the elaboration of [...] [a] Christian theology."

Christian faith in a contextually intelligible manner.[24] As a result, the theology, which emerged from this recontextualisation, differed fundamentally from its former incarnation, especially that which continued to pursue the Augustinian (i.e., Platonic) tradition. Tensions with the theology of Bonaventure, for example, which, with the exception of a few terminological loan words, refused to theologically assimilate Aristotelianism, were unavoidable.[25] The difference was so fundamental that the Church authorities themselves initially did not want to (or could not) accept this mode of theologising.[26]

Such recontextualisation cannot simply be placed on an equal footing with mere assimilation to the mentality of the time nor

[24] As is also the case for us with respect to Thomas' own thought: "If one reads Thomas then one is bound to come to the conclusion that his manner of argumentation is completely alien to us. Valid arguments for Thomas and, no doubt, his contemporaries, are no longer attractive. Nine out of ten of his arguments tend for us to be inadmissible. We would appear to have a completely different conceptual structure to that of Thomas (and the people of medieval times)." From: B. Delfgaauw, *Thomas van Aquino. De wereld van een middeleeuws denker* (Kampen/Antwerp, 1985) 205. See also H. Küng, *Große christliche Denker* (Munich, 1994) 146: "Thomas can only be understood correctly today if we submit ourselves to 'a profound experience of strangeness';" it is for this reason that the maintenance of the immediate actuality of Thomas' theology constituted the primary mistake of neo-Thomism (with reference to O.H. Pesch, *Thomas von Aquin. Grenze und Größe mittelalterlicher Theologie. Eine Einführung* (Mainz, 1988, [2]1989).

[25] See J. Decorte, *Waarheid als weg*, 182. Further p. 203, together with E. Gilson, *The History of Christian Philosophy in the Middle Ages* (London, 1955, repr. 1985) 382. Decorte paraphrases the motto 'philosophia ancilla theologiae': "Because the maidservant of the new theology was also new, all the household chores suddenly took on an alienatingly different complexion."

[26] Theses of Thomas, together with theses of the so-called 'Averroists', were condemned in Paris in 1277 by the city's bishop, E. Tempier, and simultaneously in Oxford by R. Kilwardby, the Archbishop of Canterbury, and again in 1284 and 1286 by the latter's successor, J. Peckham. Thomas was canonised and his name was cleared of any suspicion in 1323.

indeed with an unrestrained desire for innovation. B. Delfgaauw writes of Thomas' position: "The desire to find the truth and to pass it on to others is at the forefront, rather than the desire to be original."[27] Leaving behind older, neo-Platonic modes of thought, moreover, Thomas did not simply take over Aristotle lock, stock and barrel. He arrived, rather, at a new synthesis.[28]

5. TRANSITION

Having arrived at this point, it seems appropriate to offer some reflections *on the radicality of recontextualisation*. Is it the *same narrative* of God and Jesus Christ that we pass on when we engage in the development and hermeneutics of tradition? Or does tradition change? Given our fundamentally changed context, is it really possible to grasp the intention of the evangelist, for example, or the patristic, medieval or existentialist theologian, let alone to endorse what they have said? It is only via our present-day awareness and our contemporary frames of interpretation that we can hope to discern the intentions of the past. This need certainly not imply that the study of the tradition is ultimately meaningless and unproductive. It does imply, however, that what we encounter in the tradition — whatever fits or supports our insights as well as whatever strikes us, touches us, contradicts us, challenges and questions us, even that which forces us to renew our insights — is always irreducibly encountered within our current frames of interpretation. The study

---

[27] B. Delfgaauw, *Thomas van Aquino*, 17. See also J. Decorte, *Waarheid als weg*, 175, in which the author relates that Thomas ran up against both 'genuine Aristotelians' (Averroists), who maintained that he did not do justice to Aristotle — whom they read from the perspective of the Arabic commentator Averroes —, and conservative theologians "who suspected him of indulging too many and too dangerous innovations" — see also *Ibid.*, 203.

[28] For further argumentation in this regard, see B. Delfgaauw, *Thomas van Aquino*, 197-203.

of a dogmatic statement or theological text from an older context always takes place under the conditions of our present context.

The questions facing us in this regard sound radical indeed: to what extent does the context essentially determine the content and manner of our belief? Do we believe in a (partly) *different* God and Christ than the Christians of the fifth century? Even though we formally express our faith in the same God and the same Christ and even employ the same words to do so, do we still share the same history as our early Christian predecessors? Do we still belong to the same ecclesial community? Can we understand the continuity of tradition in terms other than those of family kinship? Does our unavoidable participation in a strictly historically-determined context not put insurmountable obstacles between us and past tradition? Perhaps our present context simply forces us to think of God and Christ in a different way. As such, the context can be seen to have changed to the extent that we are no longer able to perceive the same events and interpret (formally speaking) the same texts in the same manner as before. If this is true, then the consequences for theology are clearly far-reaching. It would mean, among other things, that in spite of the fact that we read the same words (and even this is a matter of dispute) we no longer read the same Bible. It would also imply that within succeeding temporal articulations people ultimately believe differently.[29] It seems that every believer or believing community from whatever era thus employs the 'same' texts and often indeed the 'same' words in its search for the ultimately incomprehensible core of the Christian faith on the basis of its own contextual awareness and interpretative frameworks. In short, this means that the identity between the

---

[29] This is not only valid from the diachronic perspective but also from the synchronic perspective to the extent that a variety of paradigms exist side by side: distinct theological currents within Catholic theology, diverse confessions within Christianity, and the variety of world religions.

stages of tradition is contracted at some indeterminate point, meaning that it can no longer be properly elaborated except in a context-bound and highly particular language. The insight involved in such a contraction, however, makes the expression of identity a difficult task, the results of which will always remain contextual, and thus transitory and never complete.

Whatever the case, once a believing community has cast the dynamic relationship between tradition and context in a new form, it continues to narrate the Christian narrative which, paradoxically enough, is to be considered both the same as before and no longer the same. Identity and rupture go hand in hand at this juncture. On the one hand, the community remains faithful to its original inspiration and continues with the same narrative precisely by giving new expression to the same inspiration in a changed context. On the other hand, it would be difficult for the same community to live their faith within the parameters of the older form of the tradition, even although many elements thereof — images, symbols, rites, narratives, terminology, concepts — have been taken up in its new expression and in spite of the fact that the older form of the tradition continues to be maintained by some members of the community.

What we have said so far, however, not only allows us to understand the fact that the tradition is undergoing a process of development; it also teaches us that our actual understanding of the tradition is also part of a well-defined conceptual horizon, a contextually-determined manner of looking at tradition. Even today, we are incapable of occupying a disengaged, independent observer's perspective. The fact that we are part of history makes such a position impossible. The discovery of plurality in the Christian tradition (on account of its development) and of the undeniability and indeed legitimacy thereof, is peculiar to our own time. It is in this sense that we are confronted with a *recontextualised* view of tradition. Such a (r)evolutionary perspective on tradition is new to the extent that other perspectives (rooted in different theological paradigms) in the past only accepted that, at most, *cumulative* development took place, evolution towards more and better.

This radical change in the way we perceive the tradition, however, is not undisputed. It is the result of the changes in context that the Christian narrative has undergone (and still undergoes) since the beginning of the modernisation process (beginning in the sixteenth century but especially in the eighteenth century), changes which also generated other conceptions of the tradition. Moreover, the very questioning of the perception of tradition and the way we should deal with it are probably central in the developments issued by the processes of modernisation. If we can consider the Christian tradition as a continuous process of development in spite of/thanks to discontinuity, then modernity's rupture with tradition draws particular attention to such discontinuity. It even leaves the present author wondering whether discontinuity in the modern period does not do away with all continuity. The change of context brought about by modernity does not so much confront the Christian tradition with new questions (similar to former context shifts), rather it presents a fundamental challenge to the very right to existence of a 'tradition-based' Christian narrative. We shall unfold this question further in our second chapter.

II. MODERNITY AND THE RUPTURE
OF TRADITION

In this second chapter we will endeavour to take a closer look at the rupture which modernity constituted for the Christian narrative and in particular for the role and perception of the Christian tradition.

To this end we will begin by sketching the basic characteristics of the cultural modernisation process — and the reflection on fundamental life-options that was engendered by it — on the basis of a number of socio-cultural and cultural-philosophical observations. We will then endeavour to determine the extent to which tradition and the concept thereof were affected by this process. We will conclude with a short analysis of Christianity's reaction to this modernisation process.

It should be clear in the meantime that we have already moved a step further. While recent analysis still employs the expression 'modern culture', the contemporary cultural climate in which we live tends to be typified rather by the expression 'postmodern culture'. What is meant by 'postmodern culture' and the extent to which this change of context has had an influence on the way we speak about the Christian tradition will be the subject matter of our third chapter.

1. The cultural modernisation process: secularisation

When we use the expression 'cultural modernisation' we are referring in fact to the process of cultural change that went hand in hand with the transition from a traditional agricultural society to a modern industrial society. One of the most significant structural developments that emerged from the sixteenth century onwards was the process of *functional differentiation*[1] whereby distinct arenas of activity took on an increasing degree of independence, concentrating themselves on the promotion of one specific social function. Autonomous arenas (referred to as sub-systems) such as science, economy, labour, politics, law, education etc., came into existence independent of the dominant and overarching traditional worldview. Each developed its own characteristic methodology, institutions and role patterns. This differentiation ultimately resulted in the gradual separation of the sub-systems from the life-world in which they functioned. While the sub-systems were initially rooted in traditional, local customs and common traditional worldviews, the process of their emancipation from these was unstoppable. Economics, politics, science, education and law, began to develop their own logic and detached themselves from traditionally transmitted religious and moral presuppositions. In so doing they disengaged themselves from their environment. This disengagement did not take place overnight, however. The traditional worldview consisted in the transmission of a particular understanding of human life and activity that was legitimated primarily by the authority of custom. The economic sub-system, for example, gradually gained independence by detaching itself from family-based roots in production and trade, thus leading to the commercialisation of role patterns and impersonal market relations.

The slowly-evolving consequences of this development are of direct significance for our analysis. A double evolution led to a

---

[1] R. Laermans, *In de greep van de Moderne Tijd: Modernisering en verzuiling, individualisering en het naoorlogse publieke discours van de ACW-vormingsorganisaties. Een proeve van cultuursociologische duiding* (Leuven, 1992) (more specifically part 1: "Culturele modernisering en verzuiling"); J.-F. Lyotard, *La condition postmoderne* (Paris, 1979); W. Welsch, *Unsere postmoderne Moderne,* Acta humaniora (Weinheim, 1987).

diminishment of the Christian religion's (and thus also the Christian tradition's) importance and all-encompassing range. The first and most important of these evolutions was that of *secularisation* that emerged as the direct consequence of functional differentiation. Secularisation must be understood from two distinct perspectives. On the one hand, the diverse sub-systems emancipated themselves from the all-embracing religious horizon and rejected every claim to religious truth within their own domain. The religious tradition thus lost its prominent role as all-encompassing source and point of reference for human values and convictions and found itself excluded from the diverse sub-systems. This development went hand in hand with a number of infamous conflicts between the Church and science, the Church and politics, etc. On the other hand, religion itself was forced to take on the form of a sub-system, developing, among other things, its own logic, institutions and role patterns. Religion came to focus exclusively on the promotion of the religious function in society, side by side with, yet distinct from, the other functions. In so doing, religion was forced to withdraw from public life, its relevance reduced to the organisation of the private arena and intimate relationships, side by side with the fulfilment of a comfort/consolation function.

A second consequence of functional differentiation was evident in what came to be known as the *generalisation of values*. Where the local community once derived its convictions with respect to truth and value entirely from its own traditions, this was now only viable (and to a lesser and lesser degree) in the private arena. The functional differentiation of sub-systems from the broader environment ultimately gave rise to a situation in which only very general norms, detached from the particular, could be considered all-embracing. Moral consensus, as a result, was only possible at highly abstract levels such as respect for the personal value of every human being. If convictions and value propositions stemming from the tradition survived, they did so detached from their traditional foundations.[2]

2. MODERNITY'S 'MASTER NARRATIVES'

The structural development of functional differentiation also left its traces in the way people looked at the world. After the all-embracing and integrating characteristic of the religious tradition had disappeared, new forms of integration were called for. The response to the call came in the form of the so-called 'master narratives' of modernity, which were given concrete form in the modern ideologies of the nineteenth century. These master narratives not only constituted a response to the disintegration of human existence into diverse sub-systems, they also established structures of self-legitimisation at the level of fundamental life-options.

The secularisation of social activity — i.e., its detachment from the religious sphere — led to a view of the human person in which *human autonomy* and thus also *human responsibility* were central. The emergence of the sciences and the advancement of technical potential, moreover, provided the modern human person with the knowledge and the instruments to take this responsibility to heart. Human responsibility and technical know-how ultimately resulted in the claim that reality was *open to manipulation*. The modern

---

[2] Jürgen Habermas describes the process of modernisation as the rationalisation of the life-world. On the one hand, sub-systems take over functions from the life-world and thereby relieve its burden. On the other hand, the traditions become reflexive within the life-world itself. Convictions and value perspectives are no longer accepted merely because they stem from the tradition. Such perspectives have to be rationally justified as yes/no propositions. Reference to custom ('it has always been so') no longer legitimates opinions concerning truth and value but rather convincing argumentation: J. Habermas, *Theorie des Kommunikativen Handelns* (Frankfurt am Main, 1981).

human person considered the development of a humanised world its primary responsibility.

Various blueprints for a better society took shape in a variety of social projects that came to be referred to as *modernity's master narratives*, each of which legitimated the human desire for progress and emancipation in its own way. According to Jean-François Lyotard, these narratives can be reduced to two types: the master narratives of knowledge and the master narratives of emancipation. According to the latter, knowledge stands at the service of emancipation.[3] The initial steps of these narratives were established during the Enlightenment (18th century). From the second half of the nineteenth century onwards they turn into major ideologies, which also determined the twentieth century. Capitalism, communism, liberalism, conservatism, positivism and so forth constituted a variety of endeavours to integrate, legitimate and steer the dynamics of differentiation. These ideologies legitimated themselves by appealing to the scientific character of their position. Typical of these 'isms' is the fact that they tended to emerge from one specific sub-system (or from the human life-world) in order to acquire a broader perspective on the differentiated whole. As such, they absolutised the logic of one of the sub-systems. Marxism, for example, employed the economic sub-system as a matrix in order to consolidate its grasp on the differentiated sub-systems in human society and culture and used the schema of basis-superstructure in order to achieve this. Liberalism grafted itself onto the liberal concept of (political) freedom in order to provide structure to the now collapsed life-world. Conservatism harked back to the premodern form of the life-world as a matrix that could encompass the world and its sub-systems in a single whole. It will be evident that such master narratives exhibited a totalising character which not only

---

[3] J.-F. Lyotard, *La condition postmoderne. Rapport sur le savoir* (Paris, 1979).

endeavoured to include society as such but also to give direction to every form of individual concrete thought and action.

A plurality of ideologies thus emerged, master narratives which tried, each in its own way, to oversee and direct the process of modernisation in line with its own specific aims. As post-traditional discourses, ideologies posited themselves on the ideological market as synthetic systems of meaning. Historically speaking, the religious sub-system also developed its own socially-oriented master narrative in competition with the other narratives. At the societal level in Flanders, as well as in many other regions of Europe, this ideologisation led to the phenomenon of *pillarisation*. Parallel to master narratives like socialism, liberalism and nationalism, Christianity created its own pillar which resulted — in Flanders — in the proliferation of an enormous Catholic network of organisations, services, associations and provisions. From birth to death this network provided the lives of its members with structure and meaning. Its concrete realisations still survive to the present day in its extensive web of Catholic kindergartens, schools, hospitals, and residential homes for the elderly, together with countless cultural and sporting organisations, trades unions, and political and socio-economic associations.[4]

3. MODERN CRITIQUE OF RELIGION AND TRADITION

The tradition was to face serious consequences as a result of this process. From a position of pre-given unquestionability — religion as the all-embracing horizon of meaning and value — religion found itself in a position of *fundamental questionability*. The various '-isms' came to treat religion as a competitor and

---

[4] J. Billiet, ed., *Tussen bescherming en verovering. Sociologen en historici over zuilvorming,* Kadoc-Studies, 6 (Leuven, 1988).

endeavoured to deny it legitimacy. Religion, on the other hand, adopted the same position towards these other ideologies, emphasising its own traditional roots and authority in face of their criticism. Radical critique of tradition and stubborn defence thereof squared off against one another as the master narratives crossed swords.

Modernity not only forced religion (and religious tradition) onto the defensive at the socio-structural level but also at the level of *fundamental life options*. For the eighteenth century thinkers of the Enlightenment and the modern thinkers of the nineteenth and twentieth centuries, religion and its tradition-bound concept of truth constituted a stumbling block to the development of science and emancipation. Master narratives of science saw religion as mere *superstition*; master narratives of emancipation considered it a source of oppression and *alienation*.

In his response to the question, 'What is Enlightenment?' (1784),[5] Kant insisted that traditional religion was the principal obstacle to the enlightenment (i.e., the movement of human persons away from the infancy for which they themselves were primarily to blame). Unconditional adherence to the tradition, according to Kant, obstructed every form of betterment and change. When it comes to human progress in knowledge and freedom, the past must never stand in the way of the present nor the present in the way of the future. "One age cannot bind itself and conspire to put the following one into such a condition that it would be impossible for it to enlarge its cognitions (especially in such urgent matters) and to purify them of errors, and generally to make further progress in enlightenment. This would be a crime against human nature, whose original vocation lies precisely in such progress; and succeeding

---

[5] I. Kant, "What is Enlightenment?," Id., *Practical Philosophy*, trans. and ed. by M.J. Gregor (Cambridge, 1996).

generations are therefore perfectly authorised to reject such decisions as unauthorised and made sacrilegiously."[6] Since adherence to the tradition limits research and progress in the present, it must be considered unfruitful (unable to give life) and thus destructive for humanity as such. The modern human person only acquires the necessary space to make progress by leaving the tradition behind. Attachment to the past inhibits human projects towards a better future. Tradition-critique and modernity go hand in hand.

From the nineteenth century onwards, the great ideologies of science and emancipation adopted an offensive strategy in their attack. The positivism of Auguste Comte, for example, considered religion as the first phase, the infancy, of human growth towards the authentic knowledge of the sciences. Liberalism underlined the individual autonomy of the modern human person at the political and moral levels against the authority of Church and state. Socialism and communism viewed religion as a conservative power at work in the oppression of the worker, a power that helped to legitimate the unjustified status quo.[7]

4. CHRISTIANITY AND ITS TRADITION: TWO REACTIONS TO THE DYNAMIC OF MODERNITY

In the historical encounter between Christianity and modernity we can discern two more or less distinct positions, each characterised by the way in which the former related itself to the process of modernisation.

---

[6] *Ibid.*, 20.

[7] Karl Marx maintains, for example, that religion is the opium *of* and *for* the people. *Of* the people, because it can thereby reconcile itself with the unbearable circumstances of its existence here and now, comforted by the expectation of a much better future in the afterlife; *for* the people, because religion is the instrument of those in power, which they use to hold the people in obedience.

A first type of reaction to the modern critique of tradition consisted in the endeavour to integrate the former without allowing the Christian faith to disappear altogether. Under pressure from modern rationality and criticism of religion, Christianity re-profiled itself in such a way that the results of modern thinking were no longer irreconcilable. Two important strategies emerge here which we can describe as *theological conformation* and *theological recuperation*. In the first place, the adherents of the Christian tradition tried to take modernity's critique of religion and tradition seriously. Wherever modern standards considered religion and tradition to be outdated and oppressive, such criticism was taken on board. Thus, what the Bible and the tradition purported to be against the natural sciences was unrelentingly suppressed or given a completely different interpretation. In just as dogged a manner as the modern thinkers themselves, those elements of religion which Kant accused of 'selbstverschuldete Unmündigkeit' were criticised and expurgated by religious thinkers. The legitimisation of this theological reception of modernity's critique of religion leads us to the second typical strategy: *theological recuperation*. Here modernity was no longer viewed as an event that was hostile to Christianity. On the contrary, it was seen as an immediate continuation of the Christian narrative. Modernity was simply recuperated at the theological level and written into the Christian narrative as the logical consequence of the 'secularising dimension unique to the Christian faith'. In this regard, the theologians of secularisation emphasised the biblical dictum that the Creator had placed creation under the responsibility of human beings. Thus, the modern passion for scientific knowledge and the construction of a better society was provided with a Christian legitimisation.

Although perhaps lacking in nuance, one might claim that modern theologians simply followed modernity's master narratives and adapted the content of faith to accommodate them. This was clearly the case with the liberal theologians of the nineteenth and early-twentieth centuries (for Catholics up to and after the Second Vatican Council) when it came to the supremacy of scientific positivism and the modern concept of emancipation at the level of fundamental life-options. The political theologians and liberation theologians followed a similar policy during the heyday of (neo-)Marxist critique from the end of the Sixties. In each instance the content and formulation of the faith shifted in line with the new perspective. Tradition was thus simultaneously viewed negatively, as coagulated past, and positively, as open to ongoing adaptation. In the context of this movement of assimilation, however, which saw the Christian narrative graft itself onto the great modern narratives of emancipation, the former came to adopt the characteristics of the latter. The first reaction to the process of modernisation ultimately resulted in a number of Christian *and* modern master narratives.

In contrast to the first reaction to the modernisation process, a second position can be discerned which might be characterised by its *complete rejection of modernity* based on the argument that modernity had nothing to offer Christianity and the belief that modernity and its presuppositions were irreconcilable with the Christian narrative. Those who maintained this position defended Christian faith in terms of its traditional content and formulation against what were perceived as the attacks of modernity. Adaptation and change, it was insisted, led unavoidably to injury and loss. Theology had nothing to gain by entering into dialogue with modernity. Modern critique of religion was seen as a delusion of hubris, the autonomy of the secular as a guilty rejection of the dependent relationship with God in which humanity and the world found their integrity. Only the complete rejection of modernity could save Christianity. Confronted with the master narratives of modernity, Christianity formulated its own *great counter-narrative* in which traditional frames of reference, formulations and contents were stubbornly adhered to in the face of every form of modern critique of religion and tradition. In the form in which it had been inherited, the Christian tradition related the true narrative about God, humanity and the world, and this was valid for everyone, past, present and future. This truth was unassailable, revealed and entrusted to humanity in the Bible and the tradition and not simply placed at humanity's disposal. The Church, and more specifically the Magisterium, was responsible for protecting the integrity of this salvific truth. The result was a sustained and inflexible dogmatisation of the historical form of the anti-modern Christian master narrative.

The two positions we have sketched are, of course, *extremes* that were seldom fully realised. Nevertheless, they offer a framework in which we can gain some perspective on the recent history of Church and theology. As a matter of fact, the reactions of the Catholic Church and its perception of the tradition, as they can be discerned through time, are fairly typical of the two modes whereby modernity and the critique of tradition were received.[8] In the first instance, the Catholic Church formulated its own great anti-modern counter-narrative, the basis and keystone of which was the historically-inherited tradition. The defence of the truth of the tradition against the insights of modern science and the emancipatory ideologies was paramount. The First Vatican Council and various encyclicals from the nineteenth and early twentieth centuries — from *Mirari vos* (Gregory XVI, 1832) to *Humani generis* (Pius XII, 1950) — are illustrative of the Catholic position. The Second Vatican Council opted, albeit with prudence, for a different approach

---

[8] A. Kohnstamm-Bodenhausen & Th. Salemink, "Dubbele waarheid in een universum van onzekerheid. Paradoxale omgang van het Vaticaan met de moderniteit in de negentiende en de twintigste eeuw," ed. H.W.M. Rikhof & F.J.H. Vosman, *De schittering van de waarheid: theologische reflecties bij de encycliek Veritatis splendor* (Zoetermeer, 1994) 154-179; T.G. MacCarthy, *The Catholic Tradition. Before and After Vatican II 1878-1993* (Chicago, 1994) especially 25-81.

and proclaimed an innovative openness towards the world. Modernity and the critique of tradition could be taken seriously without having to abandon Christianity and the tradition. Following in the spirit of Vatican II, theologians grafted the Christian narrative onto modernity, integrating modern themes such as human responsibility and freedom into their theologising. In more recent years, however, the anti-modern position has been gaining more and more ground on the waves of the crisis of modernity.[9]

It should be clear, therefore, that modern and anti-modern theologians each have a different perception of the tradition. Anti-modern theologians consider the tradition to be a pre-given whole entrusted to the Church (the teaching authority). In their view, the rationale of the tradition runs counter to the dynamic developed by modernity. While modern theologians (for the most part) likewise take the tradition as their point of departure, they also tend to emphasise the need for dialogue with modernity in order to keep the tradition alive. Modern theology is thus said to have two sources or poles: tradition and situation.

In summary: the process of modernisation elicited a dual defensive reaction among Christians, both of which are of extreme importance for the concept of tradition. In the relationship between modernity and Christianity (tradition), the *traditionalist* approach placed the emphasis on Christianity's own unique narrative and the truth claims that accompany it. Based on its own premodern past, a great Christian anti-modern counter-narrative was set up in contrast to the modern master narratives of science and emancipation. The assurance of the truth (contained in the tradition) was hereby

[9] H.J. Pottmeyer, "Die Suche nach der verbindlichen Tradition und die traditionalistische Versuchung der Kirche," ed. D. Wiederkehr, *Wie geschieht Tradition? Überlieferung im Lebensprozeß der Kirche,* QD, 133 (Freiburg/Basel/ Wien, 1991) 89-110. See also L. Boeve, "Gaudium et Spes na de crisis van de moderniteit. Het einde van de dialoog met de wereld?," ed. J. Haers, T. Merrigan & P. De Mey, *Volk van God en gemeenschap van gelovigen. Pleidooien voor een zorgzame kerkopbouw* (Fs. R. Michiels) (Averbode, 1999) 246-261.

primary. The *modernising* approach aimed not so much at a defence of the truth on the basis of the tradition but sought points of contact in the master narratives of modernity. Its adherents hoped to uphold the offer of truth of the Christian narrative by linking it with the modern master narratives. The theology of secularisation did this, for example, by insisting that modernity was a logical consequence of the Christian faith. Whatever ran counter to the modern narratives in the Christian narrative was unrelentingly eliminated. The Christian narrative became a modern master narrative.

Both positions are at fault because they each adhere to *only one single pole of the relationship with tradition.* Traditionalists overemphasise the idea of being heirs: the inheritance is preserved and passed on as a whole, undifferentiated; a creative and life-giving reception of the tradition is rarely mentioned. The modernising tendency emphasised the idea of being contextual benefactors: the inheritance was streamlined, adapted and, where necessary, corrected in the light of the modern critique of tradition. In the first instance, the tradition as a dynamic process of recontextualisation was abandoned. In the second instance, the tradition as bestower of meaning was neglected; the Christian narrative ran the risk of becoming a (legitimating) reduplication of the modern master narratives. At each end of the spectrum the essential interaction between the tradition to be passed on and the actual context (in reality or in principle) came to a halt. The strategy of adaptation gave the context pride of place and relinquished the tradition. The traditionalist strategy led to a withdrawal into a fossilised tradition and the context was rejected as sinful.[10]

[10] As we already noted in chapter 1, genuine recontextualisation endeavours to sustain interaction between tradition and context. Moreover, it presupposes a theologically-motivated critical awareness with respect to both — and stemming from the encounter of both. Indeed, the very explicitation of this critical awareness can only be the result of an actual — to be implemented — recontextualisation, whereby the — as such unavailable — critical impulses of the Christian message can only find expression by being embedded in the particular context.

III. THE POSTMODERN CONTEXT:
THE DEFINITIVE END OF TRADITION?

The conviction that 'modernity' is no longer the appropriate term
to describe the conceptual world of today and that 'postmodernity'
should take its place is steadily increasing. What then should we
understand by 'postmodern'? According to Jean-François Lyotard
— one of the best-known postmodern thinkers — postmodernity certainly does not imply that modernity is a thing of the
past. Indeed, he insists that the very opposite is the case.[1] In
Lyotard's view, we entered postmodernity at the point when the
modern master narratives of knowledge and emancipation (which
received their social form in the great ideologies) lost their legitimacy and plausibility. With the collapse of these master narratives, however, it becomes clear that they had been attempts to
direct and guide the processes of modernisation. Modernisation,
however, enjoys its own dynamic, one that continues to unfold,
detached from the master narratives. In this sense, 'postmodernity' might also be characterised as 'radicalised modernity': the
era in which functional differentiation, or viewed more broadly,
the pluralisation of the world, can no longer be kept together
under one single perspective. If the strategy of the master narrative no longer functions, however, which role, if any, can we
continue to ascribe to the Christian tradition, to the Christian narrative?

---

[1] See J.-F. Lyotard, *La condition postmoderne. Rapport sur le savoir* (Paris,
1979); *Le différend* (Paris, 1983); *Le postmoderne expliqué aux enfants. Correspondance 1982-1985* (Paris, 1986).

1. INDIVIDUALISATION AND PLURALISATION

Detraditionalisation and the construction of personal identity

From the sociological perspective,[2] the modernisation process ultimately resulted in the process of individualisation[3] according to which the social context in which the individual is rooted became increasingly detraditionalised. The specific class-based culture in which labourers, agricultural workers, the self-employed, blue-collar and white-collar workers, management and employers tended to identify themselves with one or other master narrative disintegrated. Certainties, values and norms inherited from traditions were relativised. Specific customs, lifestyles, social behaviours etc., were

---

[2] See also: R. Laermans, "Van verzuild volk naar ontzuild individu. Culturele ontwikkelingen in het naoorlogse Vlaanderen," *De gids op maatschappelijk gebied* 81 (1990) 125-147, p. 143; "Van collectief bewustzijn naar individuele reflexiviteit. Media, consumptie en identiteitsconstructie binnen 'de reflexieve moderniteit'," *Vrije tijd en samenleving* 9 (1991) 99-118; "Meer individuele mogelijkheden, minder sociale dwang? Enkele cultuursociologische kanttekeningen bij het naoorlogse individualiseringsproces," ed. W. Dumon, et al., *Scenario's voor de toekomst* (Fs. 100 jaar sociale wetenschappen aan de K.U. Leuven) (Leuven, 1993) 137-151.

[3] Individualisation as a cultural trend, and thus as a descriptive category, ought to be strictly distinguished from individualism as an ideology, from egoism as a moral qualification and so forth. In addition, individualisation should not be indiscriminately identified with 'becoming more of an individual', i.e., the acquisition of a personal identity (individualisation as a psychological mechanism). As we shall see, the process of individualisation (understood sociologically) offers structural possibilities for personal identity formation. Whether or not these possibilities are realised by (all) individuals has nothing to do with the process as such and changes nothing with respect to the structural character thereof.

The same distinction is also valid for the terms (post-)modernisation/(post-)modernity versus (post-)modernism, pluralisation/plurality versus pluralism, etc. The initial terms should be understood as descriptive while the terms ending in 'ism' stand for particular ways of interacting with the described situation whereby elements of the description are brought to the fore as normative.

no longer seen as indicators of the social class to which a person belonged. Increasing prosperity, mobility and educational possibilities, among other things, brought about a mounting degree of independence from the social context.[4]

Emancipation from bonds that were once taken for granted and left unquestioned has resulted in a situation in which every human being is given the *structurally*-subjective task of *constructing his or her personal identity*. Each individual is expected to construct his or her own identity profile by making choices from a broad selection of possibilities. This process of choosing is no longer automatically determined by one's social status or gender or indeed by the particular social cluster to which one belongs. The process of individualisation has thus led to a degree of independence with respect to the decisions one makes in the way one lives one's life. The opportunity to choose, however, often takes on the proportions of an *obligation* to choose. A world of multiple possibilities in which the individual's life is no longer worked out in advance ultimately implies that the individual has to make his or her own way. In other words, personal identity is no longer preconceived: it has become more and more *reflexive*. This does not necessarily mean that the customs, perspectives, values, norms and so forth, which

---

[4] The root causes of the process of individualisation are to be found in the centuries-old process of modernisation. Accompanying aspects hereof, which have a role to play in the process of increasing individualisation, include: (1) increased availability of education and educational level, resulting in the relativisation of the family as the primary context of socialisation; (2) increased economic capital that guarantees both material independence — thus facilitating individual choice — and the material potential to realise individual options; (3) urbanisation via the process of migration from traditional village and neighbourhood contexts; (4) significantly increased mental and geographical mobility; (5) massively expanded leisure possibilities and, to conclude, (6) the persistent rationalisation of the lifeworld via, for example, the infiltration of scientific, medical and psychological insights that undermine traditional conceptualisations and practices.

were once passed on without question, have completely disappeaed. On the contrary, they continue to function but only as part of the broad selection of possibilities from which the individual is free to choose. Those individuals, for example, who do not abandon the traditional ways in matters of relationships, family size, raising children etc., still continue to differ from previous generations because their traditional lifestyle is a matter of choice. Neither class, nor gender, nor premodern religious values and norms can claim any exclusive regulatory function in the determination of people's lifestyle.[5]

The pluralisation of the life-world

Side by side with the process of individualisation, the postmodern life-world came to be characterised by a further process, namely that of *pluralisation*. As a matter of fact, the individual's awareness of plurality is a significant point of departure in his or her reflection on matters related to fundamental life-options. The human life-world is not only disintegrated into countless fragments, human individuals also become more and more aware of the pluralisation process as such.

Radical plurality is a basic characteristic of our times. Indeed, the basic premise that the same information can be considered from a variety of completely different perspectives with equal justification is fundamental to postmodernity. Every perspective is understood to have value in itself even if mutual incompatibility as well as occasional conflict are evident. Universal and uniform perspectives no longer hold sway; the master narratives have given up the ghost. This basic experience of postmodernity can be discerned in a broad

---

[5] This also does not imply, however, that there is no longer any social influence on such decision-making, only that the quasi-automatic and unquestioned transmission of traditional class and gender lifestyles has come to an end.

variety of domains including, for example, literature, architecture, sculpture and painting, as well as cultural and scientific philosophy, economics and politics. In each of these domains we are confronted with a multitude of perspectives, language games, methodologies and conceptual theories that are often difficult to reconcile with one another. Given the fact that plurality as such persists as a presupposition of every kind of thought and deed, one is left with the inevitable conclusion that no one still has the right to claim to be in possession of 'the' truth. Postmodern critical consciousness resists in principle every claim to hegemony. Every form of universalistic pretension is critically unmasked as an absolutisation of one particular standpoint.

This pluralisation process is the *flip side* of the individualisation process. Individual men and women make use of the multiplicity of types of rationality, modes of action and existential patterns, orientational frameworks, horizons of meaning, social theories, language games, scales of value and world views as a resource, as a sort of cultural market in which they can construct their subjective identity. The very confrontation with such plurality, however, inevitably raises questions: 'What do I really want?', 'Who am I?' The individual is no longer arbitrarily driven in one particular direction. On the contrary, he or she is continuously confronted with the *reflexive* task of constructing his or her identity and with the demand to evaluate this constructed identity in light of market availability. New and different elements constantly appear on this market which call the individual's constructed identity into question time and again. Every reflexively-acquired identity is thus characterised by only a relative degree of stability.[6] Postmodernity can thus be justifiably referred to as *reflexive* modernity.

---

[6] Within the processes of identity construction, as these take place in the lifeworld, material stemming from such prospective possibilities is 'recontextualised'. Besides a market significance, cultural goods also acquire an "always specific

2. RELIGION BECOMES A MARKET COMMODITY – TRADITION BETWEEN
   NEW AGE AND FUNDAMENTALISM

It would appear that this 'reflexive modernity' has finally forced the
Christian tradition to definitively abandon its claims. If Christianity
still has a role to play, then it is only as a disintegrated and fragmented
collection of cultural values and goods which are available on the cultural market and from which one is free to choose as one goes about
the business of constructing one's own identity. Tradition, with its
claim to be a living and life-giving narrative, would appear to be irreconcilable with this new situation. Moreover, the availability of options
on the religious market continues to expand with the introduction of
elements from other ancient traditions and new religious movements.

One might summarise the situation by stating that the social significance of the tradition as a horizon of interpretation for personal
and social existence has collapsed in modernity and postmodernity.
In the process of functional differentiation, the various sub-systems
uniformly detached themselves from the overarching religious traditional horizon. What remained in terms of truth and value was
torn out of its traditional bedding. The ideologising recuperation
movements that endeavoured to restore the tradition as a factor of
integration continued up to the middle of the twentieth century.
When these movements also ran aground — in the postmodern
context — the process of individualisation and its accompanying
detraditionalisation gained momentum and the tradition as a whole
dissipated further into the background. Elements thereof ultimately
took their place on the characteristically plural *cultural market*.

'life-meaning', given that they are perpetually integrated in individual life projects,
personal biographical options, etc." (R. Laermans, "Van collectief bewustzijn naar
individuele reflexiviteit," 112). An ongoing dialectic continues to exist "between
the gigantic supply of potential 'sources of identity' on the one hand, and the
question 'who am I really?' on the other" (*Ibid.*, 114).

Is it possible, therefore, in this postmodern context, to continue to speak authentically of tradition? Reality is plural! Traditions that survived the collapse may still manifest themselves but only alongside a multiplicity of new fundamental life-options on the same cultural market. The individual is invited to construct his or her own identity on the basis of this many-sided market supply. Tradition would appear to have been reduced to one among the many religious commodities that, at the level of quality, are no longer easy to distinguish from one another. Does Christianity only have a future as a reservoir of take-it-or-leave-it fragments of meaning, as a stock of items intended to assist in one's personal religious formation?

Certain approaches to traditional Christian material, narratives, terms and customs tend to confirm this perspective. In many of the New Age movements, for example, the Christian tradition only appears to have a 'future' in what I would call a post-Christian perception of reality. We have moved on from the age of Pisces to the age of Aquarius. People autonomously determine their own religious identity on the basis of what is available in the religious supermarket. Fragments of classic religious traditions are set free from their original contexts and are combined with fragments from other traditions and elements of new religious movements. Key words in this religious supermarket include esoterism, the paranormal, gnosis, pantheism, syncretism, the occult.[7]

The image of the individual who autonomously constructs his or her own religious identity, however, is not entirely foreign to

---

[7] See J. de Hart, "Het derde milieu. Jongeren en New Age," *Kultuurleven* 60 (1993) 30-39, p. 30; R. Woods, "New Age Spiritualities: How are we to Talk of God?," *New Blackfriars* 74 (1993) 176-191, p. 177). See further: R.H. Nanniga, *Geloven in het paranormale*, ed. R. Kranenburg, *De tegenbeweging, Religieuze Bewegingen in Nederland*, 24 (Amsterdam, 1992) 99-122. A good description and analysis of occultism is offered in W. Janzen, *Okkultismus: Erscheinungen – übersinnliche Kräfte – Spiritismus (Stuttgart, 1988)*.

Christianity as it is concretely lived today. Here, too, there is evidence of the religious consumer exercising his or her right to self-determination. The result is an *à la carte* religious identity.[8] Religious communities often fall in line with this process and become 'service churches'. As we noted, moreover, the market of religious satisfaction offers chunks of traditional Christianity side by side with alternative esoteric products. Indeed, when confronted with this extended market many Christians do not immediately reject what it offers, even when it clearly does not have its roots in the Christian tradition itself. They either integrate New Age elements into their originally Christian narrative[9] or reintegrate (forgotten) elements from their own tradition that appear to connect with the New Age alternative.[10]

Others completely reject the situation that allows people to arbitrarily construct their own religious identity on an individual basis and take the opposite direction, that of *traditionalism*. Such individuals and groups tend to be profoundly critical of the postmodern processes of pluralisation and individualisation that lie behind this situation. Their primary fear is the existential uncertainty that accompanies the postmodern condition (and the ultimate loss of the Christian narrative). Traditionalists search for (and find) guaranteed truth in the (static) tradition that enables them to survive in the pluralized world in spite of pluralisation (and simultaneously to save the Christian narrative from obliteration). For them, the processes of differentiation and pluralisation lead to relativism,

---

[8] K. Dobbelaere, *Het 'volk-gods' de mist in? Over de kerk in België. Kerk-zijn in de huidige wereld - 1. Sociologische benadering,* Nikè-reeks: Didachè (Leuven, 1988); H.-J. Höhn, "City Religion. Sociologische Glossen zur 'neuen' Religiosität," *Orientierung* 53 (1989) 102-105; L. Voyé, "La religion en postmodernité," *Studies in Religion* 22 (1993) 503-520.

[9] P. van Zoest, "New Age en christelijk geloof. Een greep uit de vele publikaties," *1-2-1* 22 (1993) 365-366.

[10] See the fashionability of angels in our days: see K. Nientiedt, "Engel – gibt's die? Ein Literaturbericht," *Herder Korrespondenz* 48 (1994) 472-477.

indifferentism and nihilism. When every perspective, every option, every language game is as good as the other, then nothing is true or good anymore. In such circumstances one cannot even hazard to speak of truth or falsity, good or bad. Given such a climate, therefore, traditionalists tend to hark back to the Christian tradition as the only source of absolute truth and goodness. In their opinion, only a full restoration of the (not yet) broken tradition can hope to turn the tide of relativism, indifferentism and nihilism. Such traditionalistic positions tend to be strongly associated with much censured religious fundamentalism.[11]

As a matter of fact, both aspects of the Christian narrative's dual reaction to modernity make a *radicalised* comeback in postmodernity. The traditionalist-fundamentalist position leaves no room for creative reception as inheritor while the religious 'bricoleur' makes *tabula rasa* before constructing his or her religious identity, whatever the inheritance may have been.

3. REFLEXIVE BELONGING TO TRADITION

The fundamentalistic position would appear to be the only one to continue to profess its adherence to the tradition as such. Beyond this there seems to be no future for a truly tradition-based engagement of

---

[11] Fundamentalism is commonly described as that movement which adheres to the letter of its own (closed) tradition. As Verhack thus notes, it is "a manner of dealing (or, more correctly, of not being able to deal) with questions surrounding the *secure foundation* of a religious faith [...][,] with the problem of the 'objective uncertainty' of the faith" (I. Verhack, "Terugkeer van de religie?," *Bijdragen* 53 (1992) 152-181, p. 175). For the fundamentalist, only that which exhibits supernatural and inexplicable validity can enjoy religious persuasiveness. The fundamentalist thus submits to this inexplicable and supernatural dimension. Traditional religious texts, therefore, are not open to interpretation. They are collections of data of divine origin. See the thematic edition "Fundamentalism as an Ecumenical Challenge" (*Concilium* 28 (1992) 3) for useful information, evaluations and suggestions with respect to the question of fundamentalism.

pluralized reality. From the philosophical perspective, this is related to the pessimistic cultural expectation that a differentiation, which is no longer under the direction of the master narratives, ultimately leads to indifference. Tradition then gets lost in the market's inability to discriminate. Only when a stop is put to this situation from within a new master narrative, which claims to be able to counter the modern differentiation process, will the tradition have a chance to survive.

The everyday engagement of ordinary believers, however, contradicts this supposition.[12] It is indeed clear that the Christian individual's relationship with the Christian tradition — which saw its unquestioned and self-evident character called into question by the modernisation process — will certainly be different. Christians also participate in the individualisation process of the postmodern era and are well aware of the incontestable pluralisation that characterises the world in which they live. Christians are likewise called to construct their own religious identity. Their conscious option to enter into or remain within the Christian narrative is no longer to be presupposed. From now on, belonging to a determined (institutionally anchored) tradition must take place in the plural and reflexive (post)modern context, in the dynamic interplay between both identification with, and taking one's distance from, tradition — reliance on tradition and renunciation thereof. This presupposes a capacity to deal reflexively and productively with the tension between the task of personal-identity construction and the institutionally transmitted tradition. Entering into the tradition (and the community which upholds it) goes hand in hand with a degree of tradition and institution critique.

---

[12] For this and the following paragraphs, see K. Gabriel, "Tradition im Kontext enttraditionalisierter Gesellschaft," ed. D. Wiederkehr, *Wie geschieht Tradition? Überlieferung im Lebensprozeß der Kirche,* QD, 133 (Freiburg/Basel/Wien, 1991) 69-88; Idem, *Christentum zwischen Tradition und Postmoderne,* QD, 141 (Freiburg/Basel/Wien, 1992).

Given that no single master narrative (with the possible exception of what one could frame as today's all-encompassing master narrative of 'marketisation'[13], the postmodern face of capitalism) is still calling the shots, entry into a living tradition is gaining ground once again. It is at this point that the Christian tradition in all its richness perhaps could offer a potential for meaning and orientation once again. The modernisation process — i.e., individualisation and pluralisation — brings with it a loss of orientation. The once travelled roads have become overgrown with the proliferation of fragmented cultural products. *Even in a pluralized world, however, narratives continue to be told.* Choices made on the cultural market do not have to be merely subjective and arbitrary. Traditions that have been able to stay 'alive' in the pluralized world may have the capacity to offer some lead for individuals and communities in our pluralized society. Such traditions, however, no longer take the form of a (modern or anti-modern) master narrative, but that of a (postmodern) *open narrative.* These are narratives which are well aware that identity formation today happens in an individualized and pluralized context and draw the lessons from the fate of Modernity's hegemonic master narratives.[14] An open narrative therefore both is conscious of its own historicity, contingency and particularity, and perceives of its own meaning and truth claims in relation to the claims of other narratives.

Those who consider themselves part of such an open narrative in which they find meaning are still conscious of the pluralisation of society. They are aware that their own meaning-giving narrative is simply one among the many and that — at least at the structural level — their participation in it is a matter of choice. An open narrative must make it possible to provide a place in one's own life

---

[13] See chapter 4.
[14] See chapter 5.

for plurality, without either glorifying it or allowing it to dissolve one's life into indifference. Traditions that have the capacity to transform themselves into open narratives in our postmodern world cease to be shutters which block out the view, as is the case in various strands of traditionalism. On the contrary, they become windows that allow men and women to observe and to live in the colourful multiplicity of postmodernity.

We already noted above that individualisation and the construction of one's own religious identity do not automatically imply that mere subjectiveness or arbitrariness is the determining factor in a person's option for the Christian faith. Even when Christians are well aware of the *optional character* of their faith decision (influenced as they are by the process of individualisation), many still interpret this option as a vocation. Rooted in its very nature, the Christian faith continues for such individuals to contain a call on the part of a transcendent reality. Rooted in their initiation into the Christian tradition, those who respond to this call learn to refer to this transcendent reality as the God who made Godself known in Jesus Christ as the God of love. The structurally undeniable individual-reflexive decision to believe can be experienced in faith as a vocation, a grace, a gift. The faith decision is thus experienced from within as an obligation to choose, as an inability to do anything other than choose to believe. While the option not to believe remains a possibility for Christians, it implies (from the perspective of faith) an option for inauthenticity.

The autobiographical reflections with which the French Jesuit theologian Joseph Moingt introduces his study *L'homme qui venait de Dieu* provide a striking illustration of the changed and more reflexive relation of Christians to tradition today.[15] He writes that

---

[15] J. Moingt, *L'homme qui venait de Dieu*, Cogitatio fidei, 176 (Paris, 1993).

the first time he taught christology at the Jesuit institute in Lyon-Fourvière his course took the form of classical christological tractate (*Traité du Verbe incarné*). The method consisted of explaining the logic of the christological dogmas in the hope of arriving at a contemporary faith understanding.[16] While the method does deliver knowledge of the tradition, Moingt writes, it is not a good way to account for the tradition because it never moves beyond the closed tradition of the Catholic Church. Not only was there little distance from the received classical tradition but also little attention was paid to new developments in the culture, philosophy, human sciences and non-Catholic theology of the time. There was little hope of gaining much insight into the contemporary faith situation because the connection between the gospel and everyday reality was seriously neglected. When in 1968 Moingt became professor at the Institut Catholique in Paris and a short time later at the Jesuit Centre Sèvres, he revised his christological courses. The new spirit that surrounded the Second Vatican Council and the modern christologies stemming from German Protestant theologians played a significant role in this revision. He no longer devoted his classes to the teaching, justification and discussion of the traditional christological dogmas. In light of the critical rationality of the time, his new aim focused on giving due attention to faith in Jesus Christ. Both tradition and the modern context were part of the process.

This dialogue between tradition (knowledge of the faith) and context (critical rationality) tended in the first instance to produce

---

[16] See *Ibid.*, p. 7: "His domain [= with respect to the christological tractate] was the tradition of the Church, the history of dogma, the teaching of the Magisterium, the dogmatic propositions of scholastic authors, particularly those of the Doctor communis, St. Thomas Aquinas, and the theoretical elaborations of 'authorised' contemporary theologians. Limited and understood in such a fashion, it was possible to summarise the tractate on 'the incarnate Word' in a commentary on the dogmatic formula: 'Christ is one person in two natures'."

critical questions with respect to the Christian faith. On the other hand, questions emerged from faith itself. All these questions, all these doubts, Moingt notes, are constitutive of faith. "I learned to doubt, because knowledge is necessary if one is to doubt, and I learned to believe, because one must be able to doubt what one knows in order to know that one believes."[17] The tradition continues to play an important role in this process. It is the collective-constitutive memory of the Church that, as memory, must remain present in our reflection as the impulse and legitimation of the continuation of the same tradition. The purpose of the tradition is not to simply repeat the truth but to go in search of it. One has to inherit in order to pass on one's inheritance.

---

[17] *Ibid.*, p. 10.

PART 2

FAITH IN THE POSTMODERN CONTEXT:
OPEN *VERSUS* CLOSED NARRATIVES

'More than a million copies sold: even the Low Countries are under the Celestine spell woven by James Redfield's best-selling book. The churches are empty but nostalgia for the Garden of Eden is alive and well. Everyone today seems to have his or her own DIY faith. "We are all souls in search of our selves." ... Marketing experts from the USA have been shouting it from the rooftops for a long time: the search for meaning in life is a growth market in the nineties and in the new millennium. In more recent years the same can be said for Europe. Of course the exclusive cliques in which one can be assisted by a therapist to discover one's primal scream or wisdom from a former life, the esoteric bookshops and the house, garden and kitchen clubs are still in full swing. In the last few years, however, the phenomenon has exhibited enormous expansion. New Age with its myriad branches has become a multi-million dollar business, a hunting ground for flashy young entrepreneurs and the new professionals of the new economy. ... Money and the search for meaning are no longer the adversaries they once seemed to be [at least according to the flower power movements of the sixties]. On the contrary, the idea that "money is energy" is being proclaimed right and left. Why shouldn't we pay for spiritual growth? The members of the local fitness club have no problem with that." [1]

---

[1] Extract from a Belgian newspaper: *De Standaard Magazine* (03.04.98, p. 4 and 15) on the occasion of the success of the New Age best-sellers of James Redfield, *The Celestine Prophecy* and *The Tenth Insight*.

· *'The worst thing the traditional meaning-giving institutions such as the Churches can do is to panic and turn themselves into modern or postmodern meaning-giving multi-nationals: either by championing an imposed de-mystification by concentrating on a perfectionist moralism or by setting themselves up as clever peddlers of the techniques and signs for the construction of meaning which have been adapted to suit current tastes. Perhaps the most essential thing — and at the same time the most difficult — is to avoid entering into competition, to avoid the urge to recruit or to recover lost ground, but rather to create and to offer space for silence, prayer, comfort, reverent celebration, 'pointless' gathering, even for those who do not share the same convictions, etc. Perhaps such un-modern, intimate anti-activism is just what we need to keep the future open in relation to a past which may no longer seem familiar but which is nevertheless still ours.'*[2]

---

[2] H. De Dijn, *Hoe overleven we de vrijheid? Modernisme, postmodernisme en het mystiek lichaam* (Kapellen, 1994) 52.

IV. IDENTITY AND MEANING
IN THE POSTMODERN CONTEXT

Modernity and postmodernity have placed the Christian tradition under serious pressure. The actual postmodern context challenges the Christian narrative to recontextualise itself. Our growing awareness of plurality would especially appear to offer an important point of contact in this process. In this and the following chapters we will endeavour to elaborate such a recontextualisation step by step.

To this end we will begin by returning to a number of the most significant elements of the preceding chapter and focus on the current problem of the construction of meaning in more detail. We will examine the problem of fundamental life-options in the postmodern context at closer quarters. Is there a middle way between hardened traditionalism and ultimate relativism? Are the critics of postmodernity right when they claim that the postmodern dynamic will result in the loss of modernity's achievements, in arbitrariness and chaos? Or is it more accurate to claim that our modern world has learned the lessons of recent decades and has developed a contemporary critical consciousness? In order to answer these questions, we will turn our attention to the seemingly unavoidable temptation to cope with the search for meaning and identity in terms of a 'master narrative'. Radical plurality then tends to be either rejected or toned down by such 'master' or 'closed' identity-constituting narratives (section 1). A predominant place in this regard is set aside for the ubiquitous master narrative of 'marketisation' which paradoxically appears to make use of the process of pluralisation in order to encompass and control it (section 2). In more general terms, we can state that such narratives of rejection and disempowerment are clearly attempts to counteract the insecurity that accompanies the formation of identity in our day and age. What is true here in general with respect to fundamental life-options, is also true with respect to religion (section 3).

In chapter 5 we will take a closer look at the nature of the critical consciousness as we already practised it in our analysis of chapter 4. This will provide the basis for our further elaboration of the model of an open narrative (briefly referred to in chapter 3). In chapter 6 we will try to ascertain whether this model can be applied to the Christian tradition — the term taken in both its passive and active sense.

1. Pluralisation and the Temptation of the Master Narrative

We have already established that the process of modernisation has led to an ever-increasing pluralisation. This does not mean, however, that the postmodern condition has no place for forms of integration, for patterns which structure the way we deal with this multiplicity (in the present study referred to as 'narratives'). Although the modern master narratives of knowledge and emancipation may have lost their plausibility, narratives continue to be told. People have to live with the situation of pluralized, disintegrated reality in which they find themselves. Individuals and society, which constitute an inalienable part of this multiplicity, have to relate to it in one way or another. What is the nature of this relationship? How does the process of integration take place and what perspective do the various patterns of integration have to offer on multiplicity? Is the 'master narrative' structure still maintained or do the narratives of today have a place for a postmodern critical consciousness (which judges the modern master narratives to be implausible and untrustworthy)?

Although discredited, the modern narratives have made new attempts to extend their all-inclusive integrative powers.[1] At the same time, alternative narratives try to control and even direct the pluralizing tendencies of the postmodern world. Two approaches are evident in this regard, one that rejects plurality outright and another that tries to subdue it. All-encompassing tendencies of marketisation also represent a feature of postmodern narrativity that cannot be ignored. Are such tendencies gradually crystallising into *the* postmodern master narrative par excellence?

Narratives of rejection

While the narratives of rejection accept pluralisation as an accurate analysis of the actual situation, their evaluation thereof is roundly negative: *pluralisation is a harmful development that must be rejected.* The processes of pluralisation lead to chaos, relativism, amorality and even immorality. Other terms often associated with these processes include aestheticism, individualism, narcissism, superficiality, nihilism, cynicism, elitist hedonism, etc. *Anything goes.* Such an analysis often goes hand in hand with a programme of reintegration of plurality. These narratives can also be qualified as 'master narratives' to the extent that they — in line with the master narratives of modernity — develop patterns designed to bring plurality under control.

According to some, pluralisation can only be suppressed by going back to *the situation prior to modernity* and by embracing the old (often religious) narratives of unity once more. Only within the frameworks of such narratives can certain elements of modernity

---

[1] Illustrative in this regard are the efforts of communist and social democratic parties to redraft their political profiles (New Labour in Great Britain, the Labour Party in the Netherlands and the Socialist Party in Belgium). The formulation of the concept of 'cultural Christianity', intended to continue the legitimation of pillarisation structures beyond de-traditionalisation and ongoing secularisation (as is the case, for example, in Flanders), runs parallel to this evolution.

be ascribed any right to existence (and even granted legitimisation). The various forms of present day neo-conservatism and fundamentalism (traditionalism) constitute a good example in this regard with their rejection of modern (emancipative) fundamental life-options and postmodern plurality as pernicious and even perverse. On the other hand, however, such 'movements' often exhibit a great deal of respect for the achievements of scientific and technological rationality, even at the economic level. The rebirth of diverse forms of nationalism, with their endorsement of identity formation on the basis of ethnicity, native soil, race, etc., likewise constitute a striking example of what we mean by narratives of rejection. When these (anti-modern) narratives refer to themselves as post-modern they do so in the literal sense of the word: *after* modernity, *beyond* modernity. Those dimensions of modernity that lead to an unbridled process of pluralisation can and indeed must be stopped.

Others condemn such neo-conservatism and nationalism as a premature abandonment of the genuine achievements of modernity. They reject the anti-modern remedies because they tend to blame pluralisation not so much on modernity but rather on a degenerate and corrupt process of modernisation. It is not modernity and its struggle for emancipation and justice that is to be rejected but the corruption thereof by pluralisation, arbitrariness and the evident absence of any form of control. They insist that the *modern project* and the fruits of modernity should not be dismissed with too much haste. Rationalisation, scientific progress, social emancipation etc. remain essential elements of the dynamic that aims at a better world for humanity and social existence. Only a modernity that returns to its original project can offer a future and effectively overcome the 'crisis of modernity'.[2]

---

[2] The German philosopher and social scientist Jürgen Habermas was at the forefront in developing this position: the actual complexity of the social situation is not rooted in modernity or the process of rationalisation but rather in the corruption of modernity by the marketisation and bureaucratisation of social

Narratives of disempowerment

The narratives of disempowerment take a different route to that of the anti-modern and (late)modern narratives of rejection. Instead of trying to constrain plurality under some all-embracing narrative of unity, the narratives of disempowerment either refuse to engage in such a procedure or reject it as simply impossible. By contrast, they recognise the irreducible and irreconcilable character of multiplicity and give in to it, albeit without much enthusiasm. For such narratives, the discovery of radical plurality often spells the end of every form of utopia, every ideal or dream, every struggle for truth, justice, goodness and beauty. Radical pluralism leads to *radical relativism*; radical differentiation in this sense ultimately results in *indifferentism*. Pluralisation results in the *disempowerment of plurality as plurality*: everything is equally true, equally good, equally beautiful. If one option differs only marginally from another, why should one bother to choose?

Cynical-apathetic and *ironic-aesthetic* approaches to life both tend to take such relativism as their point of departure,[3] the former abandoning all plans for the future as pointless and futile, claiming that unrestrained postmodernity ultimately leads to disintegration, while the latter transform the same lack of restraint into a sort of blissful licentiousness, organising their lives as they see fit and engaging in every form of experimentation. The so-called 'postmodernist' philosophies of life tend to exaggerate these approaches and accentuate their normativity: the human condition is one of postmodern 'blissful arbitrariness'; 'do your own thing' is the order of the day.[4]

---

existence. For further discussion, see L. Boeve, "De weg, de waarheid en het leven. Religieuze traditie en waarheid in de postmoderne context," *Bijdragen. Tijdschrift voor filosofie en theologie* 58 (1997) 164-188, with further references.

[3] See De Dijn, *Hoe overleven we de vrijheid?*, 28-30.

[4] As already noted (chapter 3, note 3), we continue to emphasise the importance for our study of the distinction between 'postmodern' and 'postmodernity'

Concealed streamlining

On closer inspection it would seem that the narratives of disempowerment are related to the apparently *contrary tendencies of uniformity and streamlining* that are also at work in contemporary society and culture. These tendencies, however, clearly do not have their roots in the so-called postmodern processes we have been discussing but constitute instead a reaction to it.[5] While such tendencies were often already functioning in modernity under the guise of modern ideologies, they have adapted themselves to the postmodern situation. Often insidious and as good as invisible, they tend to structure diversity at every level, providing all-inclusive yet formalising patterns of integration. Given the fact that ideological justification is no longer a feature of postmodernity — partly because claims to universal truth and validity have fallen under suspicion — such tendencies simply legitimise themselves on the basis of their success and performativity: they function efficiently and offer stability. Pertinent examples include the marketisation of the lifeworld, i.e. the processes through which all of its dimensions become steered along the patterns of an economic rationality, and the influence of the media and information technology. As a conglomeration of processes, with marketisation at the helm, these tendencies form the constituent parts of what we understand to be globalisation. In each instance they exhibit strategies that opt for 'form' rather than 'content'. At the same time, variety is reduced

versus 'postmodernist' and 'postmodernism' respectively. The initial terms tend to be more descriptive while the latter terms advocate a programme in which (elements of) the descriptive terms become normative for dealing with the current context.

[5] A more penetrating study of this phenomenon can be found in L. Boeve, "J.-F. Lyotard's Critique of Master Narratives: Towards a Postmodern Political Theology?," ed. G. De Schrijver, *Liberation Theologies on Shifting Grounds. A Clash of Socio-Economic and Cultural Paradigms*, BETL, 135 (Leuven, 1998) 296-314.

to 'more of the same' and the individual to nothing more than a link in the process, like a terminal in a computer network or a television controlled by a cable distributor.

Marketisation, for example, reduces diversity in various domains to the diversity of the market whereby monetary value is more important than content. The subject becomes a consumer in the game of supply and demand, both of which are generated by the process itself. Significantly large segments of the leisure-time market and the holiday industry are part of this dynamic, even those that claim to have escaped it (e.g., adventure-holidays). Under the influence of the *media,* information is streamlined and evaluated primarily on the basis of its sensation value; television programming is driven by viewer ratings. *Information technology* digitises data and in so doing robs it of its original setting and context. Information is reduced to a series of binary codes and made available on the Web to be downloaded and used according to personal preference. In all three instances the rich diversity or, in other words, the particularity and otherness of one thing with respect to another, is ultimately dismantled. Differentiation and pluralisation are hereby transformed into *sameness and relativism*: it does not matter what one purchases as long as one purchases. Our sensitivity towards otherness thus becomes blurred and is only employed as a reason for purchase (exotic holiday destinations) or for increasing sensation (disaster tourism). Our sensitivity towards *the* other is likewise on the decline. This other has also been reduced to the familiar role of market consumer, user of the same goods and information.[6]

---

[6] It goes without saying that the disappearance of recognisable and significant identity-providing patterns lies in part at the foundations hereof. Where identity is no longer pre-established and patterns intended to support identity construction are no longer imperative, pluralisation carries with it a lack of security. Uniformisation becomes attractive, therefore, because it offers structure and an anchor

2. THE MASTER NARRATIVE OF MARKETISATION

The present-day supremacy of the narrative of marketisation deserves further analysis.[7] With the decline of the modern ideologies, this postmodern master narrative has emerged as the ultimate pattern for integration. The narrative of the market, as we noted above, does not integrate by negating pluralisation as such, but by making its result — complex multiplicity — uniform.

The primacy of economic logic

Irreducible plurality, which is metaphorically designated as the cultural market, is hereby actually organised according to the economic logic of the market. Categories such as *do ut des*, supply and demand, consumer and product, need and fulfilment, monetarisation etc., play an important role in this regard. Intrinsically-diverse

to the meaning-seeking subject. On the other hand, when this very subject loses his/her sensitivity towards the otherness of the other and plurality is reduced to 'more of the same', such patterns of uniformisation are provided with increased opportunity. Illustrative of this spiralling movement is the culture of 'the kick' that strives to increase (albeit very momentarily) the subject's experience of identity via kick experiences. The very fact that kicks appear to offer the subject heightened fulfilment in a context in which the pre-established paths to fulfilment have disappeared is what makes them so attractive. At the same time, however, given the fact that the subject lacks a sense of meaning and can see no way out of his/her situation, the kick provides an escape route. Processes of uniformisation thus provide a surrogate alternative for religion and other fundamental life-options. Something similar is at work on the other side of the spectrum: because of persistent insecurity, fundamentalism and nationalism are making a comeback by absolutising the tradition in the face of pluralisation (see below).

[7] The European Union serves as a useful illustration in this regard. Besides the more affective dream of a unified European home, economic rationality and the formation of a unified, protected European market would appear to constitute the Union's primary raison d'être, much to the irritation of those who strive for a social Europe, or a Europe of peoples and cultures.

cultural fragments become formally equated with each other: they become market goods, consumption products, items to be bought and sold. Individuals and groups emerge as buyers and sellers, consumers and suppliers. Every area of daily life is ultimately absorbed into this market perspective. Today, for example, we speak casually of the labour market, the leisure market, the marriage market, the capital market, the food market, the drugs market, the educational market. Trade fairs, exhibitions and (super)markets, on the one hand, and the multi-media, on the other, present multiplicity as available, exchangeable, and consumable. However diverse the products may be in their nature and origin, in the end they only differ in terms of cost, in function of supply and demand.

On closer inspection, therefore, pluralisation would appear to be an *objective ally* of marketisation. In fact the discovery of irreducible plurality opens up an inexhaustible source of possibilities for the market. The diversity of cultural patterns, lifestyles, ideologies and customs etc., provides the narrative of marketisation with a multitude of new opportunities for expansion: new markets, new needs, new products. This narrative is also able to rejoice in the unexpected support of recent advances in information technology that have reduced reality to a formalised stream of data. Reality is divided into manipulable, mutually interchangeable elements that can be stored without further reference to context, place or time. Traditions are thus dismantled, stripped of their location in time and space, departicularised.

Accordingly, in and through his or her options, the postmodern individual becomes entirely reduced to a consumer on the market. The loss of plausibility of the directive, and thus limiting, master narratives has resulted in the disappearance of any form of mediation between the individual and the market. The dominant narrative of marketisation has thus been able to successfully impose its basic categories on reality. *To choose is to buy.* Such a reduction has enormous consequences for the formation of individual and group identity. The distinction between individuals and groups eventually comes to be expressed financially. Leisure time, body care, car, home, trips, activities and habits, in short one's entire lifestyle is being sold and bought on the market of supply and demand. Given its influence and power, it is not surprising that advertising and the media in general play such a crucial role. Lifestyles are presented as products; the latest novelties are marketed time and again as a 'must' for the up-to-date man or woman, i.e., the consumer. Consuming, participating in the market, becomes a value in itself. The disoriented postmodern individual is an easy target for the narrative of marketisation. Identity is a question of what one can afford. In other words, one is what one is able to purchase.

While freedom is identified with the power to purchase, it is likewise limited by it. In fact, this freedom ultimately results in the hollow 'blissful arbitrariness' of the wealthy. With the absence of patterns that establish meaning, postmodern freedom remains, after the fall of the master narratives, a purely negative freedom. The loosening of traditional links has resulted in an unrestrained and random freedom — a relativism by means of which nothing can or may be of more value than anything else and everything becomes equally valuable. Identity is a do-it-yourself process. The narrative of the market embraces such relativism in order to impose its own logic on culture. Where choices are arbitrary, where identity becomes entirely relative, where orientation is no longer to be found, the logic of the market functions supreme. The narrative of marketisation has every interest in stimulating pluralisation (including relativism and the loss of orientation). Every day the media inundates the individual with overwhelming messages, cultural fragments and incentives, a torrent with which no one is in a position to cope. In this sense, the market and its all-important 'primacy of arbitrariness' becomes the unquestioned and virtually irreproachable background of life and thought.

Irreproachability

The danger of the master narrative of marketisation is its insidious and often unnoticed universalisation, whereby it is able to leave behind any external claims to questionability. At the ideological level, the narrative of the market not only enjoys virtually no resistance, it also tends to avoid presenting itself as a master narrative in the strict sense, as an ideology or confession of faith. It endeavours, rather, to seek points of contact with our awareness of, and engagement with, plurality and manifests itself as the indisputable precondition thereof, as if the economic rationality of the market was the only conceivable mediation between plural reality and the individual or society. Indeed, such irreproachability often exhibits religious characteristics.

The religion of the market

As we briefly noted in the preceding paragraphs, what counts in the hegemonic narrative of marketisation is not *what* is bought but *that* something is bought. Ultimately, the nature of the product purchased is unimportant, it is the purchasing process itself that is central, so much so that it occasionally receives a quasi-religious character, thus providing the economic narrative with religious features. New quasi-religious rituals, myths, sacraments, ethical codes and institutions arise and offer sacrifice to the marketising domination of reality: pilgrimages to Disneyland, stock market gurus, bank edifices which rise up like cathedrals and temples, the Christmas of consumption (and the consumption of Christmas), the myth of the self-made-man.[8]

---

[8] See L. Boff, "The Market and the Religion of Commodities," *Concilium* (1992) nr. 3, ix-xiii.

Both sociologist Rudi Laermans and philosopher Lieven De Cauter have studied elements of the all-encompassing consumer society in contemporary culture and have disclosed its religious features. Laermans focused his attention on the production and consumption of body fashions and health fads and concluded that health can be considered a new religion: the cult of beauty and of the body can be justifiably described as a secular religion, especially when examined in light of the increasing power of the media and the beauty industry.[9] In a similar manner, De Cauter asserts that tourism is becoming an inextricable part of capitalist consumption: 'We not only consume food, drink, washing machines, detergents, films and books, we also consume monuments and landscapes.'[10] Cultural tourism, he notes, 'inconspicuously replaces former collective rituals and meaning-giving systems', to such an extent that we might be correct in describing it as a 'a new form of religiosity'.[11] In and through the consumption of 'body styles' and touristic curiosities, as well as remnants from the (distant) past, present-day men and women are in search of significance, identity, and meaning. The religious dimensions that the consumption process appears to have acquired find their roots here. In this manner, the only narrative to reveal *de facto* that it is still capable of integrating fragmented reality is thus confirmed and left unquestionable.

[9] See R. Laermans, *Individueel vlees. Over lichaamsbeelden* (Amsterdam, 1993) 35.

[10] L. De Cauter, "Transcendentaal toerisme. Een causerie," Id., *Archeologie van de kick. Verhalen over moderniteit en ervaring* (Amsterdam/Leuven, 1995) 182. De Cauter offers a more radical formulation a few pages later: the contemporary individual encounters life in the fashion of a tourist; the touristic model of consumption determines the relationship between the individual and his/her environment.

[11] *Ibid.*, 185-186.

3. THE CONSTRUCTION OF IDENTITY AND MEANING AS THE PROBLEM

All of the narratives discussed so far attempt, as we have noted, to provide an answer to the problem of identity and meaning in the current situation. Such endeavours are characterised by the loss of plausibility on the part of the modern master narratives of integration and an emerging awareness of radical plurality in all areas of life, including the religious and the ethical. Individuals and communities are thus increasingly confronted with fundamental questions of identity.

Identity at risk

Individual and collective identity was once assured by the master narratives offered by religion or social ideology. Our present-day awareness of plurality, however, makes the limits of our own narrative (personal identity) all the more clear and the confrontation with plurality (with the other) all the more complex. In a situation of plurality and conflict, people learn to consider their own fundamental life-options and the sources of meaning and identity in their lives — in short: their own narratives — as particular, unique, bound to place and time, and limited in perspective. One's personal narrative offers a more and more specific view of reality, one that cannot be generalised and can certainly no longer claim to have 'the' truth at its disposal. Absolute certainty and absolute truth are an illusion. Plurality and conflict create a situation of *uncertainty and instability*.

Both religious *do-it-yourself-ism* (see the many forms of New Age) and *traditionalism* (anti-modern and modern) constitute answers to this situation of 'on-going uncertainty'. Both constitute narrative modes that aim immediately at identity as such. The traditionalist is caught up in the dynamic of rejection and tends to entrust him- or herself unconditionally to a pre-given narrative of certainty and truth. At the same time, such a narrative often possesses institutional mechanisms in order to safeguard itself from the hostile outside world (a strong leader, a closed community, a strictly enforced discipline, etc.). Dialogue is suspended, ongoing uncertainty locked out. Only one narrative leads to true life. Religious 'bricoleurs', in their turn, use a different strategy in their search for immediate identity. In the absence of a pre-given narrative, they are likely to look for intense experiences of confirmation, reconciliation, wholeness — experiences which result in an intensification of the 'I'-consciousness: '*I am alive!*'. In doing so they hook on to the culture of the 'kick'[12] in which a spiral of cascading thrills provides the individual with the assurance that he or she is not going to drown in the current of events, that he or she is not just 'more of the same' but ultimately 'different'.[13]

Taking everything into consideration, both the traditionalist as well as the 'bricoleurs' are looking for a safe and secure home, for protection against plurality's implication that his or her identity is open to question. Inherent vulnerability is immediately disposed of and any potential sensibility towards the other, which constitutes the foundation for the possibility of an 'open narrative', is likewise neutralised. Otherness is immediately *functionalised*: either demonised in the black and white, good and evil world-view of the traditionalist or reduced — and thus subjugated — to (exotic, esoteric) material subservient to one's own momentary invention of one's identity. Multiplicity and otherness are not taken in their own right and do not constitute an appeal for one's own narrative and identity.

---

[12] On this matter, see chapter 5.

[13] The kick is a limit-experience that attempts in the present to gain certainty amidst a more enduring, ongoing uncertainty, thus stability amidst instability. Due to its momentary nature, each kick requires a subsequent, stronger kick in order to arouse the identity-giving intensified I-experience once again when the previous kick is extinguished.

Religion between rejection and disempowerment

In as far as religions themselves have formed master narratives by analogy with, or as a reaction to, the master narratives of modernity, they have likewise come to share in the postmodern loss of credibility suffered by the narratives they sought to emulate or replace. The ultimate relativisation of personal narratives with respect to dominant narratives of every kind has been a serious blow for many individuals and communities. They are left to struggle with questions surrounding their particular religious narratives and the latter's (continuing) capacity to offer direction and orientation in situations of insecurity and instability.

The approaches to the reality of plurality proposed by both religious fundamentalism and New Age constitute examples of the aforementioned narrative patterns of rejection and disempowerment. Religious *fundamentalism* condemns pluralisation and exorcises it in the name of an all-embracing master narrative with its roots in the supernatural. *New Age* loses track of the specificity of the other encountered in the midst of multiplicity. The other represents nothing more than a new and alternative way to shape one's personal religious identity. Religion as such is thus drawn into the master narrative of marketisation.

Religious plurality manifests itself in the form of a market. Traditional elements from one's own religion and those of others are stacked side by side in the religious supermarket and made available — undifferentiated — to the religious consumer. This has taken place because religion still enjoys the capacity to fulfil a useful function on a market that operates according to the requirements of supply and demand. In as far as a religious need continues to exist in the individual and the community — a need which might be more generally described as a longing for harmony, consolation, wholeness — the market fills the gap, making religious and para-religious products available to the hungry consumer, products which pretend to satisfy this need. This segment of the religious market consists of a conglomeration of older indigenous and exogenous religious traditions together with a diversity of newer religious items.[14] Despite their incredible diversity, these religious goods tend to be characterised by their consumability, availability, manipulability, exchangeability. The 'religious' individual is deluded into believing that he or she is capable of composing his or her own religious identity according to his or her own personal options. Churches that have endeavoured to re-identify themselves as 'service churches' tend likewise to fall into the same market-orientated functionalisation of religion.

4. AN ESCAPE HATCH?

It would seem that the real challenge facing us today is to quit the strategy of the master narratives and take plurality seriously. Indeed, it is precisely in the context of irreducible multiplicity that we encounter the radical otherness of the other. Plurality exists where the other cannot be reduced to the same. One is thus able to recognise that plurality need not imply that one's personal narrative — a unique way of confronting and living with multiplicity — is passé and should therefore be abandoned. It remains equally

---

[14] This includes a pluriform multiplicity of traditional religious rituals and experiences, meditation techniques, positive thinking, faith healing, natural diets, mysticism, yoga, hydropathic cures, acupuncture, astrology, Jungian psychology, biofeedback, extra-sensory perception, spiritism, biological gardening, ancient mythologies, archaic nature cults, witchcraft, freemasonry, Cabbalism, herbal medicine, hypnosis, oriental miracle-books, iridology, cosmic kneecap-massage, graphology, reincarnation therapy, clairvoyance, telepathy, macrobiotics, ufology, and the like (e.g., R. Woods, "New Age Spiritualities: How are We to Talk of God," *New Blackfriars* 74 (1993) 176-191, p. 177).

clear, however, that particular narratives can no longer claim to be able to embrace plurality in any exclusive way. The recognition of plurality implies the recognition of the irreducible other. Types of narrative that are able to respect the radical otherness of the other and avoid the tendency to try to overpower and ultimately master plurality might rightly be styled postmodern.

V. TOWARDS AN OPEN NARRATIVE

Theological recontextualisation demands a thoroughgoing analysis of present-day postmodern critical consciousness. In the preceding chapter we discussed the flip side of the postmodern processes: the narratives of rejection and disempowerment and their inability to respect plurality. In our analysis we suggested that this inability was due to a lack of awareness of the irreducible otherness that accompanies plurality. It is from the very confrontation with this otherness, however, that one's identity construction and one's personal narrative is challenged and can be given a new and unique profile.

In the present chapter we will further elaborate the basic characteristics of this contemporary critical consciousness. Our first step will be to examine in what way the experience of the other can be analysed as a postmodern mode of experience (section 1). Based on this increased sensibility towards the other we will develop the model of the 'open narrative', — a mode of narrativity to be specifically distinguished from the 'master narratives' we have been discussing so far (sections 2-3). In the following chapter we will investigate whether our model, as an expression of present-day critical consciousness, can provide an adequate opportunity for a recontextualisation of the Christian narrative in our postmodern context.

1. THE EXPERIENCE OF THE OTHER MAKES THE DIFFERENCE

The culture of the kick

If we are to believe what we read in the proliferation of *life-style* magazines that crowd the shelves of our newsagents and bookstores

the *culture of the kick* would appear to have become the primary
rage of postmodern experience, with bungee-jumping[1] and reality-
TV as the examples *par excellence*. Kicks imply sensation, stimu-
lus and intensified thrill, and postmodern people seem to be
addicted to them. In their hunger for experience they look for more,
for quicker and more intense experiences. It is as if an accumulation of kicks is needed in order to assure people that they are not
going to be submerged in the indifferent stream of everyday events,
that they are 'different' and not just 'more of the same'. The kick
heightens one's self-consciousness in a kind of condensation of the
present. It becomes a moment of confirmation for the insecure Ego,
a powerful awareness that 'I am here' and 'I am not going to drown
in the incomprehensible and directionless pulp of multiplicity'.

Why this quest for an accumulation of kicks? Why this frenetic
desire for the transgression of boundaries? What does the 'kick'
teach us about contemporary men and women? Perhaps it shows
us first of all that in postmodernity *no real experience* is possible

---

[1] See De Cauter, *Archeologie van de kick*. Paradoxically, the consolidation of
self-consciousness in the kick experience takes place against the background of
the elimination or lessening of consciousness. The kick accompanies intoxication,
that is, a situation of being beside oneself. The intoxication of speed has become
trite, commonplace - this is the 'strategy of acceleration': ever-faster transporta-
tion, faster computers and computer networks, fast-changing images in video clips,
zapping and video games. By way of illustration, one might reflect on the horrific
road accidents that take place every weekend as the result of a cocktail of alco-
hol, drugs and speed. Included in this group are also spectacular events such
as bungee jumping. This is an extreme kick, a flirting with the unconscious state,
with disintegration. Besides the intoxication of speed, there is also the intoxication of deceleration or the 'deceleration strategy'. This is a reaction against the
modern feeling of being hurried along by time, against the continuous push of the
modern rhythm of life by the stress of the 'urgency of time', the pressure of 'time is
money', and by perpetual restlessness. For example, in a state of stupefaction brought
on by the pure distraction of ecstatic dancing under narcotics, the 'ego' is able to free
itself from the 'ego' that at the same time is the prisoner of hurried frenzy.

because of the flood of stimuli that confronts our everyday existence and the collapse of integrating narratives. Real experience presupposes a narrative, a memory and a platform from which we give an experience a meaningful place. In this sense, therefore, the kick is really nothing more than a pseudo-experience, a non-experience, and the accumulation of kicks an effort to make us forget about the absence of the narrative. This effort to forget brings us to a second point: the flight towards the kick is the reverse side of the human *longing for identity* and desire for happiness. A world without a narrative, "without connections and correspondences, without relationships to people and things, without a network of meanings, is an unhappy world. In the moment of exhilaration the world becomes rosy once again [...] The factually meaningless world becomes flooded with associations, images and meanings. Everything looks back. The world has regained its soul. Such an experience of meaningfulness is one of fulfilment. [...] Of course, the balance is precarious. The happiness of the imagination soon changes into an imagined happiness and the imagined happiness turns into real misery."[2] The kick is an effort to hold on to one's own identity in the midst of fractured multiplicity as it threatens to elude our grasp. As a boundary experience, the kick provides a moment of self-consolidation, a here-and-now endeavour to obtain assurance amidst insecurity and stability in the midst of instability.[3]

---

[2] *Ibid.*, 77. See also on 'falling' (as in bungee jumping): "The violent participation in the kicks associated with speed is [...] paradoxically enough, a final argument: humanity at its core is vulnerable. Falling is the ultimate form of surrender. It is searching for experience in spite of the overabundance of banality and the ongoing overdose of distraction. Understood as such, the kick is an unconscious, and barely reliable form of 'shock therapy' against a poverty of experience" (pp. 169-170).

[3] To the extent that general cultural developments first resonate with young people, the culture of the kick has tended to manifest itself primarily in such circles. In the culture of the kick, the search for identity, for a story to live from,

Otherness experienced as alterity

Perhaps we are incorrect in reducing the postmodern boundary experience to that of the kick? Our discussion so far would appear to suggest that more authentic contemporary boundary experiences are not so much experiences of self-consolidation, self-assurance, self-affirmation, immediate experiences of identity (I have arrived!) but, rather, experiences of alterity, experiences of something 'other' that calls our identity into question ('This is not me!', 'This is beyond me!', 'This is where I encounter the limits of my understanding, of my empathy!'). These are experiences in which the ego senses itself to be approached by the other, experiences of being called away from the acquired certitudes of one's own narrative, experiences of a breakthrough, interrupting the ongoing security of one's personal narrative.

Characteristic of the postmodern boundary experience is the sense that things do not tally, that we are not masters of our own existence, that we are limited and contingent, that life is full of risks and that the narratives of security that once desired to dominate and control were unable to fulfil their promises and, moreover, have done a great deal of damage. Such postmodern boundary experiences do not simply appear out of the blue; they are always rooted in the concrete, in the here-and-now. They are radical events that tend to erupt dramatically, tearing open and shaking our existing narratives, identity constructions and certitudes. Examples include the narrative of the Christian mission in Rwanda that crashed against its own boundaries when the Hutus slaughtered the Tutsis on a massive scale; the narrative of the failure of the welfare state when a dangerously sick child is not given

consists of an accumulation of successive stimuli, without reaching the formation of a real identity. The desire for sense and meaning, love and warmth is expressed, nevertheless, in the continuous frenetic search.

assistance because the operations he needs are too expensive and have little chance of success; the United Nations narrative of human rights and democracy when diplomatic (and military) intervention in Angola, Somalia and ex-Yugoslavia fails to produce lasting results; the narrative of the democratic system when it faces the electoral resurgence of extremist right-wing political parties and government scandals that seriously damage people's faith in politics and politicians. Apart from the boundaries encountered at the wider social level, we also run up against boundaries in our personal stories when, for example, the fundamental confidence of parents is disturbed by the accidental death of their child, when a friend or fellow student decides to end his or her life, when one observes the cruelty that children can exhibit towards one another or when a love story between two people begins to disintegrate and ends in mutual hate. While it is clear that men and women often have to deal with negative experiences that force their own narrative to its limits, there are also positive experiences: experiences like the birth of a child, the blossoming of a friendship or love relationship, the success of a cherished welfare project, the intense solidarity one can experience in a supportive community or our surrender to the overwhelming aesthetic beauty of someone or something. All such experiences are rooted in an incomprehensible sense of fullness that has the capacity to extend our boundaries. Time and again such boundary experiences, both positive and negative, challenge our ongoing narratives to turn outwards, to become open narratives.

Boundary experiences that challenge us to open up our narratives are far from being mere kicks or immediate identity experiences. Rather, they are confrontations with alterity. While kicks have to be sought after and accumulated, experiences of alterity often just happen and cannot be produced. They are experiences of a *strangeness* that we are often unable to accommodate within our own particular narrative, experiences we find difficult to deal with and equally difficult to dismiss. Our sensitivity towards the irreducible other goes hand in hand with doubt and alienation. As boundary to our own identity the other engages us. By responding to the challenge of such experiences of strangeness and otherness we allow ourselves to be touched by what they reveal and ultimately become witnesses to that. Our surrender to the claims of strangeness and otherness demands an unpossessive kind of modesty that refuses to reduce the other to the self. Although identity is ultimately to be found here also, it is never immediate: it is only when one experiences the continuous call to abandon the closed privacy of one's own narrative that one can discover an open individual or communal identity.

It may be justifiable to refer to such alienating, interruptive and demanding boundary experiences in more classical terms as postmodern experiences of transcendence.

2. THE KEY TO POSTMODERN CRITICAL CONSCIOUSNESS

Recent sensitivity towards the otherness of the other has drawn the attention of a significant number of postmodern thinkers, philosophers who point out that a different kind of sensitivity has emerged in the midst of our awareness of irreducible multiplicity.[4] Indeed, this irreducible multiplicity implies otherness as such, irremovable otherness that cannot be reduced to a single narrative nor subsumed within a particular totalising perspective. Whatever we do to encompass otherness within a single narrative, it will always place itself

---

[4] For further elaboration, see L. Boeve, "Theologie na het christelijke grote verhaal. In het spoor van Jean-François Lyotard," *Bijdragen. Tijdschrift voor filosofie en theologie* 55 (1994) 269-295; and "Critical Consciousness in the Postmodern Condition. A New Opportunity for Theology?," *Philosophy and Theology* 10 (1997) 449-468.

beyond our grasp. Sensitivity towards the other in his/her/its irreducible otherness lies at the basis of what we might refer to as postmodern critical consciousness, which consists of our reference to irreducible otherness and our ultimate witness to that otherness.

More explicitly, this means that every (closed, master) narrative that aims at the authoritarian reduction of multiplicity on the grounds of its own premises (thus stripping the other of his/her/its otherness) is open to criticism. From the postmodern perspective it would appear that only those narratives which admit to the specificity and limitedness of their own perspective and which witness to the impossibility of integrating the remainder are worthy of any claim to legitimacy.[5]

3. THE MODEL OF THE OPEN NARRATIVE

Such 'postmodern' narratives, which allow themselves to be affected by postmodern critical consciousness (and thereby provide it with concrete form), are perhaps best referred to as 'open narratives'. We have already insisted on the fact that *people continue to tell stories*, even in the contemporary context. People continue to make choices and they do not do so in a groundless, arbitrary way. The choices people make are related both to their everyday lives — what to eat, how to spend one's leisure time, relationships with friends and colleagues, whether to submit one's tax returns accurately and on time — and to more fundamental matters — career choice, relationship with one's partner, questions surrounding the beginning and end of life, important options in one's experience of

---

[5] For the following paragraphs see L. Boeve, "Bearing Witness to the Differend. A Model for Theologizing in the Postmodern Context," *Louvain Studies* 20 (1995) 362-379; "Critical Consciousness in the Postmodern Condition. A New Opportunity for Theology?," *Philosophy and Theology* 10 (1997) 449-468.

sexuality, intimate relationships, and so on. At times, highly specific, deeply rooted, conscious and explicit values, sensitivities, emotions, arguments and rationalisations determine this process. At other times the process is influenced by less conscious, less explicit, less profound considerations. The same is even true for those who maintain that life has no meaning beyond enjoyment or suffering. This combination of factors, which inevitably affect the choices a person makes, can be characterised as his or her 'narrative'. What then constitutes such a narrative as an 'open narrative'?

The *model of the open narrative* is a conceptual exercise designed to explicitate what it means for a narrative when it is able to integrate the critical consciousness of our times. There is no such thing as *the* open narrative as such. As a model, rather, it stands for a combination of characteristics and criteria that allow us to clarify, evaluate and perhaps criticise various societal and individual narratives. In what follows, we will present the open narrative as a narrative structure that takes the actual situation of plurality seriously, that has the capacity to make critical judgements, and that offers the means to structure our own personal and collective narratives in an 'open' fashion. The first step of our presentation illustrates the specifically reflexive framework that characterises the model of the open narrative. The second step will focus on the three-part structure of the open narrative itself.

First step: the framework

Our awareness of plurality and our sensitivity towards the irreducible other that accompanies it enjoy pride of place in our model of the open narrative.

(a) In the first place, this implies the recognition of the fact that life is made up of a multiplicity of narratives and that no single narrative has the right to claim that it can transcend this multiplicity. An open narrative is always aware of the *incontestable plurality* in which it has its place. There are no observers any more, only participants.[6]

(b) This initial datum leads us directly to the awareness of the *particularity* of our own narrative. Our narrative is not *the* narrative about humanity and the world in which we live: it is *our* narrative. It is always a specifically-situated narrative, bound to a community in space and in time. In short: our narrative is a historically and contextually determined and determinative perspective on reality. A Christian is neither Buddhist, Muslim, atheist, agnostic nor someone who is simply searching, someone collecting 'kicks', or even someone crippled by his or her indifference towards the world. Every position on the field of fundamental life-options is that of a situated participant. Many people are becoming increasingly aware, moreover, that their personal identity could have been structured by a different narrative. Our identity, our belonging to a narrative (and to the extent that our narratives develop further in and through our participation, the narratives themselves) have a degree of *contingency* about them, something accidental, something closely related to the context in which we find ourselves. It could all have been different.[7] We will return to this notion of contingency and its consequences for the truth question at the end of the chapter.

---

[6] In principle this is also valid for every form of reflection on plurality and thus for our conceptual exercise presented here. The fact, however, that this does not mean that anything whatever can be said should be made clear by the following elements of the framework.

[7] The structurally-optional character of our fundamental life options corresponds to this at the societal level. As we noted at the end of chapter three: even when Christians experience their faith as a vocation — and are indeed unable to experience it otherwise — it remains an option in the structural sense. When the Christian narrative recontextualises itself as an open narrative, it will also be obliged to leave room for reflection on this optional character. See further in chapter 6.

(c) Insight into the contingent particularity of our own narrative need not necessarily lead to complete relativism. Indeed, the position of the relativist remains attached to that of the observer. The fact that our narrative is always *our* narrative and that we cannot abandon our narrative and withdraw to the observer's post, already implies an important and unavoidable distinction between our narrative and other narratives, narratives that only relate to what is uniquely ours on account of their otherness. On the contrary, our awareness of the uniqueness of our own narratives compels us anew to take them seriously: our belonging to a narrative is not something we can simply bracket out of our lives, it forms rather our perspective on life, a perspective that might change with the passing of time but is never outdated. An open narrative is aware that it should be taken seriously on its own grounds.

(d) Furthermore, the plural field of fundamental life-options is far from static. The multitude of particular narratives that constitute this plural field are in full movement, caught up in a dynamic game of challenge, interrogation, confrontation, threat and conflict. In and through the same challenge and conflict, however, occasional mutual exchange, profound learning processes and even paradigmatic shifts can take place. Plurality does indeed imply conflict and irreconcilability. Narratives are challenged time and again to relate to plurality. In line with what we have outlined above, we can affirm that narratives are particularly challenged by the position they take with respect to the irreducible *otherness* (concretised by other narratives) that manifests itself as the interruptive boundary of one's personal narrative.

Second step: the structure

With the final point of the preceding paragraph clear in our minds, we can now proceed to the second step in which we will endeavour to further elaborate the *three-part structure of the open narrative* and thereby explain how this key to postmodern critical consciousness operates. Although the three structural dimensions of the open narrative are presented separately, the one nevertheless implies the other, thus making them difficult to distinguish. Indeed, their very interwovenness testifies to the open character of an open narrative.

(a) First of all, an 'open narrative' is generated by an *open sensitivity towards otherness*, a specific extraordinary and cultivated sensitivity towards that which interrupts. This basic attitude expresses itself in our capacity to be open to strangeness, otherness, the unexpected. It implies that we are attentive to boundary experiences, interruptive events, marginality, experiences that reveal that our particular narrative is not all-inclusive. It likewise implies that we must learn to open our eyes to discontinuities, to what is going on at the boundaries of our particular narratives, serving to interrupt them. It calls for an attitude of trusting submission, as it were, which runs counter to our absolute desire to secure and insure ourselves against the unexpected. It demands the disruption of our natural tendency to include the harmless and exclude all forms of alienating newness. In short, it concerns a basic attitude of openness, susceptibility, and vulnerability, i.e., on the one hand, a sensitivity for 'what is happening', and on the other hand, a fundamental refusal to immediately integrate 'what is happening' into one's own narrative.

(b) An open narrative offers witness to otherness as it manifests itself in view of the narrative's openness and thereby simultaneously recognises its own boundaries.[8] With respect to one's own specific and concrete narrative, and no matter how impossible it might seem, an open narrative attempts to express its *interruption* in words and deeds, and in life as a whole. The very encounter with

---

[8] This second dimension follows immediately from the first since the basic open attitude itself implies an evocative recognition the other.

otherness that cannot be made our own, structures our particular narrative. Caught up in its own particularity, our own narrative is thus broken open in order to give witness to that which in principle already escapes our (necessarily particular) witness. By pointing out differences in fundamental ethical attitudes and lifestyles, for example, we draw attention to our own narrative while simultaneously underlining its limitations: there is more to religion/ethics than our religion/ethics. By continuing to point to the otherness of God, the Christian perspective is both confirmed as a particular perspective (or point of access) and revealed to be highly specific, one perspective among many.

(c) Our sensitivity towards and witness to the other become operational in what might be described as the *critical praxis of an open narrative*. The interruption of the other nourishes a critical consciousness that takes form in intensely *self-critical* and *world-critical* judgements and actions. This critical praxis of the open narrative is located at the level of the choices we make. It makes us attentive to the otherness of the other(s) and instils a resistance to negate such otherness (e.g., when the other is reduced to the object of *my* satisfaction in a sexual relationship or when God becomes the absolute and immediate legitimisation of *my* truth ['Gott mit uns']). In concrete terms, this praxis can also take shape in the (attempted) refusal to participate in the master narrative of marketisation, for example, no matter how difficult such a refusal might be in the present day and age. Where the other is restlessly included or excluded, and thus not respected in his/her/its otherness, our sensitivity towards the other gives rise to a critique of closed narrative patterns.

From model to reality

As we noted above, these three structural elements are interconnected. It is in the very praxis of the open narrative that our basic openness towards the other and our witness to otherness become real. While this structure does not exist in itself, it is given concrete form in a variety of highly particular narratives such as — *quod erit demonstrandum* — the postmodern, recontextualised narrative of Christianity. We already insisted that *the* open narrative does not exist as such.

Many existing traditions and fundamental life-options, particular narratives among which one might include the Christian narrative, may have the capacity to foster this sensitivity for otherness and to provide an *openness* towards the other in their own narrative context, thereby restructuring themselves as open narratives. Besides the basic open attitude towards the other, the elements of witness and praxis should not be forgotten: all three elements must be allowed to take shape within the context of a particular narrative. Such a narrative provides a level of continuity that can survive the interruptive discontinuity of the other. Otherness only exists because there is particularity.

Besides the particular, narrative dimension of the open narrative, attention is due to the dimension of openness as such which is the focus of much postmodern critical consciousness.

(a) It is this openness that generates a genuine mutual *tolerance* and *dialogue* between people of different religions and fundamental life options. Although every form of all encompassing and reconciling meta-narrative may be beyond the bounds of possibility, the recognition of reciprocal kinship within the context of the open structure of one's own narrative (which leads to the appreciation rather than the abolition of particularity[9]) remains a possible outcome.

---

[9] See, for example, the conversations between Muslims and Christians on the occasion of the 'breaking of the fast' of Ramadan on Thursday January 13th, 1999. During a morning show on Flemish Radio, a woman gave a report on a meeting that took place the previous evening. The woman was involved with an ecclesial movement striving for a true multi-cultural society and had been invited by a Moroccan community in Brussels to celebrate the 'breaking of the fast'. The same community upheld the tradition of organising a festive meal every evening after

(b) It is this openness that should enable particular narratives to deal with plurality and otherness in a *non-totalising way*. Given the lessons learned from the loss of plausibility of the master narratives of modernity, it would appear that respect for otherness or the absence thereof constitutes the ultimate criterion for enabling us to distinguish between totalising and less totalising narratives. Only thus can the resistance offered by the latter sort of narrative to the former be said to have any degree of reflexive plausibility. A sharp distinction between the two sorts of narrative, however, is far from evident: self-criticism remains a primary condition for open narratives.

(c) It is also this openness that must offset the postmodern slogan '*anything goes*' together with every form of *relativism*. Indeed, these 'master narratives of postmodernity' tend likewise to be unable to take the other in his/her/its otherness seriously, assuming him/her/it to be simply 'more of the same'. Only when concrete particular narratives are seen to be concerned with the otherness that ultimately escapes them and are able to discern the presence of this otherness in the concrete other who confronts them, will they avoid being submerged by particularism and contextualism.

sundown during the month of Ramadan, to which non-Muslim guests were also invited. The woman reported that the conversation around the table quickly became serious and absorbing, especially when religious themes such as the importance of 'fasting' and Muslim/Christian relations were introduced into the discussion. She was surprised to note, for example, that the discussion surrounding 'fasting' tended to accentuate the differences between Islam and Christianity, even though at first sight both groups appeared to maintain a similar tradition on the issue. Far from relativising matters and concluding that fasting is fasting whatever form it takes, the group preferred to respectfully recognise these differences and the unique value of each approach. The woman pointed out, in addition, that the Christians present at the discussion, living in a increasingly secularised Flanders, were even moved to question the earnestness of their own faith experience in this regard: was their experience of fasting, for example, sufficiently authentic? "Truly an unexpected and far-reaching experience," she concluded.

(d) Finally, the degree to which a plurality of narratives and no single narrative determines our identity and those of our communities, perhaps allows us to suggest that, in our present circumstances, a *multitude* of 'small open narratives' can give form and clarity to our relationship with plurality and the other.

4. THE QUESTION OF TRUTH

Some are bound to argue, however, that our relinquishment of the observer's perspective ultimately implies a profound relativism with respect to the question of truth. It is evident that open narratives do not lay claim to an all-encompassing objective truth as such. Indeed, the very impossibility of integrating the other implies that truth is no longer the point at issue for a single all-encompassing narrative let alone a plurality of particular narratives. While this need not mean that everything is true — and truth as a result is no longer a question worth discussing — it does imply that truth is no longer exclusively bound to the 'truth *content*' of a narrative. It is more a question of *living in the truth*, of relating to the truth that no particular narrative can exhaust. Narratives must point to the truth and give witness to it. Narratives *live in the truth* when they are able, from within their own particularity, to point to the elusive other, to that which continues to escape them, to that which demands witness and invites the sharpest self-criticism at one and the same time. In other words, truth is a matter of relating appropriately to the intangible Truth, of giving witness to this Truth in the full awareness that its is ultimately inexhaustible, incomprehensible and inexplicable.[10]

---

[10] See L. Boeve, "De weg, de waarheid en het leven. Religieuze traditie en waarheid in de postmoderne context," *Bijdragen. Tijdschrift voor filosofie en theologie* 58 (1997) 164-188.

5. CONCLUSION

Even after the disintegration of the master narratives, particular traditions continue to be important. The choices we make on the cultural market are not merely arbitrary, they are driven by often barely recognised and indeed barely recognisable narratives (often master narratives). In a pluralized world, traditions are capable of surviving as living traditions, of recontextualising themselves in such a way that they are neither submerged by plurality nor hardened against it. As such, they remain capable of establishing meaning and offering direction at both the individual and collective levels. Moreover, the recontextualisation of traditions is perhaps necessary if we are to resist the relentless advance of the master narrative of the market that remains one of the few to have survived the devastation of established narratives by postmodernity. In this regard, sociologists point out that elements from older traditions — which are mostly rooted in inherited wisdom (reservoirs of *savoir-vivre*) — can serve to derail the market and resist the abuse of technology and human tinkering with society and the future.[11] The challenge of religious and ideological fundamentalism likewise makes a reflection on the way in which traditions can continue to function a necessity. In the following chapters we will focus our attention on the Christian narrative in particular and determine whether it is capable of recontextualisation in the actual postmodern context.

---

[11] See in this regard A. Giddens, "Living in a Post-Traditional Society," U. Beck, et al., *Reflexive Modernization. Politics, Tradition and Aesthetics in the Modern Social Order* (Cambridge, 1994, repr. 1995) 56-109.

VI. A CHRISTIAN OPEN NARRATIVE?

In this short transitional chapter we will hold up the Christian narrative against the contemporary critical consciousness that we described in the previous chapter by developing the model of the open narrative. Our intention here is not to determine whether Christianity itself has become a master narrative — as we did, for example, in part one of our study — but to examine the possibility of an open Christian narrative. Are the specific sensitivity towards the other and the characteristic critical consciousness of our time structurally recognisable within the Christian narrative? We will follow this line of questioning further in part three of our study where it will become apparent that, within an in-depth attempt at recontextualisation, the question of a 'Christian open narrative' unavoidably leads to the question of a 'theology of the open narrative'. By way of introduction, we will offer an analysis of the consequences of accepting the plural context for a recontextualisation of the Christian narrative.

1. INTRODUCTION: RECOGNISABLE PLURALITY

Christian individuals and Christian communities are no less attentive to the irreducible fact of religious and ethical plurality than their fellow men and women. They are becoming increasingly aware that other religious subjects and communities — both within Christianity and outside it — through their own specific religious mode of existence are in search of religious fulfilment with equal intensity and authenticity, albeit in an irreducibly different way.

Here, too, the awareness of *plurality* and the corresponding mindfulness of one's own, irrepressible *particularity* go hand in hand.[1] In the religious world, however, plurality is often associated with conflict, confrontation and the absence of reconciliation. This is clearly the case when we examine relationships between the various religions. The Christian concepts of Incarnation or Trinity, for example, remain inconceivable for Jews and Muslims. The personal God of Christianity cannot be reconciled with the complex emptiness espoused by Buddhism. Those who believe in resurrection or reincarnation find it well-nigh impossible to accommodate the materialist argument that death spells the definitive end of human existence. At the same time, elements of discord are also tangible within the various religions and Churches. Many Catholic and non-Catholic faith communities, for example, find the present hierarchical structure of the Catholic Church problematic. Difficulties arise with respect to questions of the ordination of woman as well as ethical convictions concerning the beginning and end of human life. Besides these more (media-) sensitive points of conflict, however, differences of opinion and confrontation form a part of the

---

[1] See J. Leman, "God dienen te Brussel. Een onderhuids tapijt van los aaneenhangende knopen," *Kultuurleven* 62 (1995) 7, 32-39. Leman offers a survey of the various forms of religious practice one can encounter in a major city such as Brussels. With respect to Christianity he distinguishes "a variety of parallel circuits, depending on whether one is dealing with [...] Catholics, Protestants, Anglicans, Greek Orthodox, Syrian Orthodox or anomalous Christian sects (such as the Jehovah's Witnesses); and within each confession depending on whether one is dealing with natives, migrants, refugees or 'sans-papiers'" (p. 33). Besides Christianity, Judaism constitutes a recognisable group among native Belgians and there is evidence of a native, middle-class penchant for eastern forms of spirituality. Non-native Belgians tend to be of Buddhist or, more likely of Muslim persuasion, varying according to their place of origin. While their residence in Belgium often results in a reorientation of their religious positions in line with the Belgian context, there is also evidence of counter reaction resulting in various forms of fundamentalism.

day-to-day reality of religious communities at both the organisational and individual levels.

The place of the Christian tradition in a plural context

The pluralisation of the arena of religious and other fundamental life-options clearly necessitates a renewed — systematic — *determination of the place of the Christian narrative* with respect to its own history and the contemporary copious supply of alternative narratives and narrative fragments. Both the external and the internal location of what is commonly held to be the Christian tradition (and in so far as this tradition is still being passed on, the Christian narrative) are viewed differently in the contemporary context. Our perception of the plural situation has in fact led to a number of new insights into (1) the diachronic and (2) the synchronic character of plurality both inside (a) and outside (b) the Christian narrative tradition.[2]

In the first part of our study we already noted that theologians have been aware of the *diachronic plurality within the Christian tradition* (1a) for some time. In the history of tradition there is no continuity without discontinuity. On account of the sequence of historical contexts in which it found itself, the Christian narrative took on a variety of new — often mutually irreconcilable — forms. Those who take the plural context seriously — including its religious dimensions — are also aware of a *synchronic plurality in*

---

[2] How can we understand 'tradition' in such a way that it becomes capable of denoting both internal and external plurality? 'To denote' in this regard does not simply mean 'to legitimate'. It is not a question of providing theological confirmation for the variety of distinct Christian narratives but rather of the theological elucidation of a legitimate plurality: our reflection will serve as a search for criteria that can be employed to determine when and how justice is being done to the plurality of traditions and contexts in Christian narratives. A recontextualisation of the Christian narrative in dialogue with the concept of the open narrative must also constitute an essential element in our response to this question.

which the Christian tradition is conscious of its place (2b). The existence of other religions, worldviews, value perspectives and so forth — not all of which can be immediately espoused — have made Christians aware that their narrative is only *one* among the many.[3] This synchronic plurality is also evident *within the Christian narrative itself.* Indeed it might be more accurate to speak of Christian narratives in this regard (2a). While the existence of a variety of Christian Churches constitutes irrefutable evidence of synchronic plurality, the diverse forms of living and experiencing the Christian tradition (recontextualisations) within the Catholic Church and the multiple contexts in which it finds itself clearly exemplifies the same situation. The young Churches of the so-called Third World, together with the various contexts of the First World, provide the received tradition with a unique, contextually-integrated countenance.[4] It is likewise becoming more and more evident that an *external diachronic plurality* (1b) existed in the past side by side with internal diachronic plurality. Throughout the history of the Church, heresies and deviations from the orthodox tradition that were rejected at the time often turned out to be meaningful recontextualisations of the Christian faith in well-determined

---

[3] See chapter 9.

[4] We are confronted here with the explicit question as to how internal — both diachronic and synchronic — plurality can be conceptualised without avoiding the radicality thereof. Is it still possible to speak of *the* Christian tradition? Is unity still possible within the plurality of Christian traditions? A *family relationship* will certainly continue to exist because every contemporary Christian narrative ultimately subscribes to the Christian tradition as it has been passed on to us up to the present. Specific figures — in the first place Jesus Christ — narratives, words and deeds that were capable in the past of bearing witness in an always particular and contextually determined manner to the self-revelation of the unarticulable God, thereby providing foundation to the Christian community, continue to be constitutive for the faith community and binding for those who call themselves Christian, although such narratives tend only to enjoy real significance when they are recontextualised in one's own particular context.

contexts. Research in the history of theology, for example, has shown that many Gnostic ideas exercised a significant influence on the development of orthodox Catholic dogmatic teaching while the Gnostic movement as such was condemned as heretical.[5] Indeed, it is often the case that perspectives rejected by one century were valued as orthodox tradition in another. As already mentioned,[6] some propositions of Thomas Aquinas, for example, were condemned three years after his death in 1277 while the man himself was declared a saint in 1323 and even given the title 'doctor ecclesiae' in 1567, in the midst of the Counter Reformation.

2. SENSITIVITY TOWARDS THE OTHER: A RECOGNISABLE MODE OF CHRISTIAN EXPERIENCE?

Is the postmodern experience — and its implied critical consciousness with respect to the master narratives — *recognisable* to those who consider themselves to be part of the Christian narrative? Whatever way we respond to such a question, such individuals are nevertheless implicated in a *twofold* manner in the criticism of the master narratives. To the extent that Christianity in its dogmatic claims and historical manifestations pretended to be speaking for God in a too direct and exclusive way, and thus proved itself to be lacking in the necessary degree of restraint and modesty we referred to above, it is possible to recognise the patterns of the master narratives therein: the claim to be speaking and acting 'in God's name' quickly turned into the ideological claim, 'God is with us', 'God is on our side'. On the other hand, potential points of common concern remain to allow a renewed dialogue between the Christian

---

[5] See H. Küng, *Das Christentum. Wesen und Geschichte* (Munich, 1994) 173-187.

[6] See chapter 1.

faith and the actual context: Christianity owes its very existence to the dynamics of a God who revealed Godself to humanity in history without becoming identified with humanity and history. The Christian narrative is one of a God who calls us to continual conversion and to the rejection of every form of sin, suffering and oppression. Upon closer inspection, it would almost appear that the Christian narrative exists *by grace of* boundary experiences and experiences of alterity. In the very experience of alterity, the believer recognises the elusive God who always beckons further. A number of significant biblical narratives, metaphors and categories would appear to underline this point: the call of Abraham, the Exodus tradition, the figure of the Prophet, the Pilgrim, the Suffering Servant, Mount Tabor, the Resurrection and so forth. The Jesus narrative as such would appear to be the narrative *par excellence* that refuses to be 'closed'. What the religious and civil authorities wanted to bring to a close with the event of the Cross, the disciples experienced as newly and radically 'opened' by God in the resurrection. Even when the Christian narrative refers to the experience of alterity as God's self-revelation in Jesus as *love*, it remains difficult if not impossible to steer it towards (premature) resolution and closure. In making such a reference, the Christian narrative does not intend to cloak conflict and lack of reconciliation with the 'mantle of love'. It insists, rather, on a radical turnabout, a praxis of openness towards the other, towards the poor and the suffering, towards the very ones in whom God has made himself manifest as the Other (Mt 25,16ff.). The God of Jesus of Nazareth is the God of the interruptive (grace) event, the God who calls us beyond harsh inflexibility and closedness. It would certainly be worth the effort to further examine these implications at a theological level.[7] Indeed, it would seem possible to maintain theologically that the Christian

---

[7] See the third part of this monograph.

narrative can only be authentic when it structures itself as an open narrative: a narrative that allows itself to be interrupted time and again by a God who gets involved in history but does not let God-self be captured by it.

One would be seriously mistaken if one were to assume that every boundary experience, every experience of alterity should be considered a (veiled) religious or even Christian experience. Such experiences of 'transcendence' are not *per se* religious. Much depends on the nature of the narrative in which experiences of transcendence take place — the nature of the narrative that allows itself to be interrupted. There can be *no religious experience without some (however small) religious context, foundation, tradition or narrative.*[8] Where there is a certain degree of continuity there is potential for fertile (discontinuous) experiences of transcendence: we need a narrative that we can break open, a narrative that can be energised by experiences of transcendence.[9] Our reflections on the

---

[8] With respect to the relationship between religious experience and religion (religious tradition), Vergote cautions against the understanding of religious experience as the origin of religion whereby priority is afforded to experience over forms of religious expression. The opposite is rather the case: "The religious person is not religious because he/she first has a religious faith experience. It is because religious language speaks of the awe-inspiring, beneficent or fear-inspiring other, because the human person in all his/her humanity enters into communion with the other divine reality in rites and rituals, that the divinity is so real for him/her, that he/she also affectively experiences the various aspects of the divinity." See A. Vergote, *Cultuur, religie en geloof* (Leuven, 1989) 55.

[9] This is an important datum for our reflection on the relationship between faith and culture. It is too easy to continue to presume — in our proclamation of the faith, for example — that there is a mutually borne and mutually supported correlation between both: that experiences rooted in our daily lives, for example, such as the birth of a child, the love of a partner, suffering and death, can still be experienced and explained in a virtually unmediated manner in terms of the Christian narrative (in spite of the fact that the majority of people in Flanders still tend to turn to the Church in order to confirm such experiences in the context of ritual). Indeed, the opposite is the case in a lot of instances: the evident plurality

culture of the 'kick' made it clear, moreover, that experiences of the other can only bear fruit when they are taken up as part of an existing narrative, not as a confirmation thereof but as a disruptive challenge.[10]

3. CONTEMPORARY BELIEF IN THE CHRISTIAN MESSAGE: TOWARDS A CHRISTIAN OPEN NARRATIVE

It has become apparent from the first and second parts of the present study that the Christian narrative can only avoid the temptations of traditionalism and relativistic progressivism where Christians and their faith communities have the capacity to give due respect to the interplay between tradition and context in their recontextualisation of the message of faith they have received and wish to pass on.

Recontextualisation is — *grosso modo* — a *two-step* process, although sharp distinctions are difficult to make. It requires, on the one hand, a capacity to engage in a confrontation with contextual critical consciousness. On the other hand, however, and perhaps more importantly, it demands the pursuit of a contextually-anchored

of explanations of experiences refers Christians to the specificity of their own sensibilities and interpretations. For further discussion of this point, see section 3 of the present chapter.

[10] This has consequences, for example, for the conception of youth ministry. Young people participating in postmodern culture may experience on certain occasions the alterity Christians refer to in their narratives. Lack of continuity, however, is often responsible for the transformation of such experiences of alterity into a frenzied search for boundary-breaking experiences (kicks) as experiences of identity. Nevertheless, where a degree of continuity is available, i.e., a narrative community, it is evident that such experiences of the claim of the Other can provoke youngsters to establish a life-rooted faith engagement. See S. Van den Bossche, "Youth, Liturgy and Postmodernity," *Questions liturgiques/Studies in Liturgy* 79 (1998) 122-151.

understanding of our Christian faith, i.e., the development of a theology for today. In other words, the Christian narrative should not merely become an open narrative because the context demands it but rather because it discovers itself — in terms of its own particular narrative — to be an open narrative and is able to offer theological justification of this discovery.

Up to this point we have focused our attention on the first step in the process, namely, that of 'context shift' and its consequences for our perception of the Christian narrative. Dialogue with contextual critical consciousness teaches Christians in the first instance that their faith is, culturally speaking, a *particular narrative* among other narratives. As such, the Christian narrative enjoys its own perspective on reality (which cannot be grasped without some degree of perspective): Jesus, confessed as the Christ, whose story, witnessed to by the apostles, teaches Christians that the mystery of reality is called Love. More concretely this means that, structurally speaking, Christians in our present day context are *opting* for a specific narrative (and narrative community) that the context as such does not support.[11] Dialogue with culture no longer leads to the construction of a sort of common denominator (an all-encompassing consensus) but rather to the recognition of the specific and unique identity of the Christian faith. This means, among other things, that faith and life no longer overlap: 'life' in our present-day culture has become a highly ambiguous concept. It likewise

---

[11] This certainly need not imply that the Christian narrative must distance itself from every form of truth claim. It does imply, nevertheless, that it can no longer claim *to possess the truth as such*. In the context of plurality and inspired by the claim of the o/Other, the Christian narrative can no longer simply identify itself with *the* truth, it must experience itself as engaged in a precarious relationship with the truth, as *feeling its way in the truth*. While one's particular narrative is not abandoned, it is stripped of its hegemonic pretensions and thus becomes a perhaps genuine witness to the *Deus semper major* (= the God who is always greater). See, in that regard, chapter 8.

implies that 'God' is only to be included in the definition of 'human being' for 'those who believe in God'. Human boundary experiences and experiences of alterity are no longer automatically perceived as Christian experiences of God's involvement with humanity. Even for Christians, experiences are often only interpreted in terms of the Christian narrative *a posteriori*, upon reflection and with hindsight. If one forgets this, one will very likely arrive at a merely human narrative, which is nothing more than the duplication of another narrative and in essence has little to do with the Christian narrative. At the bottom line, it is familiarity with the Christian narrative and integration into the Christian community that make Christians Christian.

The Christian faith, moreover, cannot claim an *absolute* (observer's) *perspective* since this would lead, of necessity, to totalitarianism. Contextual plausibility can only be gained when it structures itself as *an open narrative*, as a narrative that has learned to perceive itself as a respectful, particular witness to radical otherness (constitutive of the otherness of the concrete other) and that is capable of developing a praxis of the open narrative (implying sensitivity towards the other, witness to the other, self- and world-criticism). It goes without saying that this will have far-reaching consequences for the way narratives and narrative communities are to function.[12]

It should be clear by now that while dialogue with contemporary critical consciousness can potentially lead us to the boundaries of a faith engagement, it cannot take us beyond the 'leap of faith'. Nothing in the context can give foundation to Christian faith. In other words, the belief that God has come close to us in Jesus cannot be rationally determined nor enforced, it remains an act of

---

[12] This implies, among other things, a model of the Church that resolutely rejects — both externally and internally — the patterns of the master narrative and in which narrative and community can become authentic witness in a variety of forms, under the critique of the God who has revealed Godself as Love.

the will, a surrender that, especially in our present-day context, is often accompanied by recurring doubt. This does not mean, however, that faith calls for a (fideistic) leap into the irrational. On the contrary: it is precisely in the dialogue with contemporary critical consciousness that theologians can discern the patterns and conceptual models that in turn, when theologically received, can demonstrate the rationality of the faith. It is at this level that the unique character of the Christian narrative can be reflexively clarified for contemporary Christians.

While a Christian open narrative can (and should) be provided with contextual foundations, this can only be done legitimately on theological grounds. Does the structure of the open narrative also enjoy *theological validity*? Is it conceivable for Christians to understand the Christian narrative as a particular witness to the 'other' who/that as 'event' continually interrupts the narrative and challenges us to develop a critical praxis? What place does God have in such a scenario? In the third part of our study we will show that the very structure of the open narrative offers promising possibilities for making our relationship with God and the place of Jesus Christ contextually and theologically reflexive.

PART 3

FOUNDATIONS OF AN OPEN
CHRISTIAN NARRATIVE

———

'In the first place there is the silent and discrete (re)discovery that faith is something of a pilgrimage, that it calls for options and decisions, that one has to give it time. The pilgrim is aware that what is essential is not to be found in familiar institutions, rather it is revealed 'elsewhere', in the spiritual autobiography of other men and women, for example, or in an unknown culture or a new (even physical) sensitivity towards oneself or renewed access to foundational writings. Many a pilgrim has experienced that the stripping bare of 'the old narrative' can offer direct existential inspiration.

In the second place there is the 'model' of the convert. Conversion is the result of a turn or reversal, a moment of grace, the eruption of the Spirit in a person's life. The convert is so taken by the faith that he or she perceives it all at once in its entirety as it were. He or she is impressed by the liberating experience that he or she has been grasped by the faith and not the other way round. He or she experiences being a Christian as a melody that accompanies the day [...].

For the person who thus believes, faith is more a source of inspiration and motivation than a doctrine or code of behaviour. Faith is not lacking in content or style, it is something that can be stirred by inspirational source texts and by the invigorating example of the prophets and the saints. At the heart of such a spirituality lies friendship with the poor. It is not those who lack wealth who remind me how my culture is a threat to humanity but the 'naked other'.[1]

'Woe to you, scribes and Pharisees, hypocrites! For you tithe mint, dill and cumin and have neglected the weightier matters of the law: justice mercy and faith. It is these you ought to have practised without neglecting the others. You blind guides! You strain out a gnat but swallow a camel!

Woe to you, scribes and Pharisees, hypocrites! For you are like whitewashed tombs, which on the outside look beautiful, but inside they are full of the bones of the dead and of all kinds of filth. So you also on the outside look righteous to others, but inside you are full of hypocrisy and lawlessness.

You snakes, you brood of vipers! How can you escape being sentenced to hell?'[2]

[1] P. Vande Vyvere, "Welke gemeenschap zal welk geloof dragen? De Vlaamse kerk tussen cultuur- en keuzechristendom," ed. L. Boeve, *De kerk in Vlaanderen: avond of dageraad?* (Leuven, 1999) 77-99, pp. 92-93.

[2] Mt 23,23-24.27-28.33 (NRSV).

VII. JESUS: INTERRUPTING ON BEHALF OF GOD

In the third part of our study we will focus our attention on the theological recontextualisation of the Christian narrative in the actual context. Two important questions will guide our analysis: an we speak on theological grounds of the Christian narrative as an 'open narrative'? What then are the theological consequences of such an affirmation?

In the present chapter we will answer these questions on the basis of a study of the foundation of the Christian narrative: faith in Jesus Christ. The Christian narrative tradition does not simply tell a story about the relationship between God and humanity, its primary aim is to confess that God has definitively revealed Godself in a specific human person, Jesus of Nazareth, Jesus the Christ. This is what constitutes the unique character of Christianity. Some might argue, however, that this very specification immediately and firmly closes the door to every form of openness. Does this claim concerning Jesus of Nazareth, as we know it from the gospels, not make such openness *a priori* impossible? How do we deal with the witness of the New Testament authors concerning Jesus as the Son of God? What should we do with Jesus' own words: 'I am the way, and the truth and the life. No one comes to the Father except through me' (Jn 14,6)?

In chapter eight we will focus on the specificity of the Christian faith in God. Together with the present chapter, it constitutes a foundational reflection in the direction of a 'theology of the open narrative'. One important question remains concerning the relationship between an open Christian narrative and other (world) religions. In chapter nine we will determine what kind of theological consequences might result from the recognition of religious plurality together with their effect on our evaluation of religious truth claims.

1. INTRODUCTION: MODELS AND IMAGES OF JESUS IN THE POSTMODERN
   CONTEXT

A specific characteristic of Christianity and its followers is the fact
that their narrative in one way or another can always be traced back
to the figure of Jesus of Nazareth, confessed as the Christ. Christians
believe that God, in Jesus, has approached humanity and its history
in a salvific manner and that God continues to do so. Time and again,
in every historical period and context, Christians are engaged in a
search for the best way to express their faith and trust in Jesus in
prayer, confession and reflection. They are on the lookout for
words, images, models and metaphors to facilitate the affirmation
and attestation of their faith experience: God saves in Jesus Christ.

The Christian use of language in this regard does not differ from
other forms of religious language. Whenever people speak of those
unique moments of encounter between the human and the divine
their language fails them. Words refuse to describe, and limit themselves to being reference points to that which ultimately resists
description. Words *evoke*, call to mind, give witness to, refer, create images. Religious images, however, not only draw our attention
to a reality that resists description, they also imply a personal call,
a vocation; they make a strong appeal. They not only provide
insight into our faith, they also quicken our faith and lay claim to
it. They challenge us to engagement, to discipleship. Those who
refer to Jesus as the 'prophet', for example, are not only placing
him in the prophetic tradition of the Jewish people that called them
time and again to conversion, they also admit to an acceptance of
prophetic judgement upon themselves. An image not only offers
insight, it implies action; it not only influences us at a cognitive
level, it also addresses our attitudes, our way of living.

Such models, images and metaphors frequently have their roots
in the surrounding context in which Christians live. Many of the

images employed by the Evangelists for Jesus, for example, have their origins in the Jewish tradition. The Anointed, the Lord, the Son of Man, Lamb of God: each image is an attempt to show that Jesus is the fulfilment of the expectations of the Jewish people. Other images of the Christ were employed against the background of the Greco-Roman context in which the first Christian communities began to take shape: Jesus Christ as heavenly prince is clothed in the purple attire of a Roman emperor; as Word, Logos, Jesus is given a more philosophical (and cosmological) interpretation in a context dominated by Hellenism. The great Councils, such as those of Nicea (325), Constantinople (381) and Chalcedon (451), likewise alluded to Jesus Christ by employing more philosophical categories.

Even today, Christians continue to be confronted with the question 'But who do you say that I am?' (Mk 8,27) and their responses usually employ the images of Jesus they have inherited from the tradition as their point of departure. A number of these images, however, no longer appear to function with the same efficacy as before. The confession of Jesus as 'king' (clothed in purple), for example, or as 'Son of Man' or 'expiation for our sins' may have its place but it presupposes a profound initiation on the part of the believer in the potential significance of such images. The final image in our brief list of examples makes this abundantly clear. In his *Cur deus homo?*, Anselm, Archbishop of Canterbury, asks himself why God became a human person and how we should understand redemption in the crucifixion of Jesus Christ in this regard. Why redemption through the Cross when all sorts of alternative possibilities could have been used? To facilitate his meditations on these complex questions Anselm was inspired by the then dominant Germanic conceptual images of fidelity, respect and obedience due to one's local prince or king, which themselves constituted the foundation of the feudal social order at the time and its associated legal system. His meditations thus led him to propose the following image of the Christ: *Christ on the cross became the expiatory satisfaction for God's honour wounded by the sin of humankind.* In so doing, Anselm was offering a reinterpretation of an image taken from the letter to the Hebrews, namely, Jesus Christ as expiatory offering for our sins, against the background of his contemporary context. His argumentation runs as follows: God's honour has been deeply injured by the Fall. In the Fall, moreover, humanity defaults on its debt of obedience and trust to God its Lord and Creator. In such circumstances, and in line with Germanic legal rationale, restoration of God's honour can only be achieved by atonement. Should restoration remain wanting, then the guilty have to be punished (*aut satisfactio, aut poena — either atonement or punishment*). The guilt of humanity, incurred in the Fall, is so immense, however, that humanity alone is incapable of restoring God's honour on its own. Humanity in its entirety is thus condemned to everlasting punishment in hell. Only via the substitution of God's own, albeit innocent, Son as expiatory offering was it possible to decisively restore God's honour and save humanity. In short, just as atonement under feudal compensatory law implied the restoration of the Lord's or Prince's honour and led to a restoration and confirmation of the social order, so Jesus Christ's atoning death on the cross restored the order of creation that had been injured by sin. It is from this perspective that the death of God's Son on the cross is not to be seen as a sign of God's extreme cruelty but rather as a sign of God's supreme mercy and charity. Only thus can humanity regain a just relationship with God and escape the punishment of eternal damnation.[1]

As the above example illustrates, the differences between our *actual context* and the context in which many images came into

---

[1] G. Greshake, "Erlösung und Freiheit. Eine Neuinterpretation der Erlösungslehre Anselms von Canterbury," Id., *Gottes Heil Glück des Menschen. Theologische Perspektiven* (Freiburg/Basel/Vienna, 1983) 80-104.

existence are clearly substantial. This explains to a degree why they fail to exhibit the same capacity to take hold of us in any immediate fashion. As was the case with the shifts in contexts in the past, Christians have to look today for new images, images that, side by side with traditional images, have the power to evoke the appealing significance of Jesus Christ. It is this very process that we call *recontextualisation*, the present-day fruits of which must include new images of Jesus that not only have the capacity to offer insight to Christian men and women but also to call them to engagement.

In the following paragraphs we will attempt to develop a new and contemporary image of Jesus based on a study of the gospels. This is not only intended to justify our claim to view the Christian narrative as an open narrative but also to show that the Christian narrative can only function in an authentic manner as an open narrative. It should become clear, moreover, that, for believers, *Jesus is the very paradigm of the open narrative*. In his life and person, Jesus presented and — in light of the witnesses of the gospels — continues to present to us what it means to exist in/as an open narrative. As a matter of fact, the evangelists go so far as to present Jesus as *God's interrupter*, interrupting closed narratives on behalf of God.

Two questions will guide our reading of the earliest literary witnesses to Jesus (questions to which every 'Jesus model' ultimately provides at least an implicit response): 'What does Jesus *do*? What does he *say* about *himself*?' and 'Who *is* Jesus? What do *others say* about him?'. In other words, we will first examine the narrative *of* the 'earthly' Jesus, his words and deeds as presented by the evangelists; we will then discuss the narrative *about* Jesus Christ who, for the evangelists, is the risen Lord, the Jesus who suffered and died on the cross and rose again on the third day. Given the status of a gospel, however, it will become clear that such a division is far from absolute: the narratives of the evangelists concerning the 'earthly' Jesus cannot simply be distinguished from the confessional statement 'Jesus is the risen Lord'. In section four of the present chapter we will elaborate on the way the evangelists gave witness to the one they confessed to be the Christ.

2. JESUS AND THE PRAXIS OF THE OPEN NARRATIVE

The gospels provide adequate indication that Jesus' narrative not only takes on the contours of an open narrative, but that Jesus himself also propagated a praxis of the open narrative and acted accordingly. In this regard, we will return to the three structural elements of the open narrative: the basic attitude of openness, the witness to the other who challenges and calls us to openness, and the critical consciousness of self and world. In what follows we will examine a number of gospel pericopes and investigate how they bear witness to the praxis of the open narrative. In the first instance we will focus on the third structural element in light of Jesus' *critical-liberative demeanour* which unmasks closed narratives and transforms them into an open narrative directed towards his Father. At the same time, Jesus offers those victims who had been silenced by the closed narratives that dominated their context the chance to speak up and invites them to participate in the open narrative that he himself proclaims and of which he himself is the example. As a second point of interest, we will briefly discuss Jesus' *explicit witness* (kerygma) to God as the Other who makes an appeal to us. We will examine the parables that speak of the kingdom of God in this regard. In both instances, basic attitude and witness, our attention will be drawn to the call to discipleship, the call to personal participation in the praxis of the open narrative. Finally, we will devote a few words to the starting and culmination point of Jesus' praxis and witness, namely his *fundamental attitude of contemplative openness* to his Father. This last point should make it clear that all three structural elements that typify Jesus' praxis of the open narrative are mutually interwoven to such a degree that they cannot be treated in isolation.

The critical-liberative power of Jesus' open narrative of God's love for human persons

An illustrative pericope that deals with the critical-liberative power of the praxis of the open narrative is that of the woman caught in adultery who is brought before Jesus and is reduced to an object of juridical dispute (Jn 7,53-8,11).[2] The sequence of verses in this pericope is highly revealing. According to the logic of the Mosaic law, the observation 'this woman was caught in the very act of committing adultery' is directly associated with the judgement: 'she must be stoned' (Lev 20,10, Dt 22,23-24). This logic, however, is broken open in a revolutionising way by Jesus' response: 'Let anyone among you who is without sin be the first to throw a stone at her', upon which the woman's accusers depart one by one. Jesus then restores the woman's right to speak ('Woman, where are they? Has no one condemned you?') by liberating her from the logic of sin and punishment: 'Neither do I condemn you. Go and sin no more'. The closed narrative of the law — which is what the law had become — is radically undone of its closedness by Jesus and thus restored in its referential power.

Jesus dismantles closed narrative structures at a variety of levels in this pericope. The law received by Moses from God and

---

[2] For background and commentary on this periscope, see: G.R. Beasley-Murray, *John,* Word Biblical Commentary, 36 (Waco, 1987) 143-147; M.-E. Boismard & A. Lamouille, *L'évangile de Jean,* Synopse des quatres évangiles, 3 (Paris, 1977) 215-217; R. Schnackenburg, *Das Johannesevangelium,* Herder Theologischer Kommentar zum Neuen Testament (Freiburg/Basel/Vienna, 1965-1975) II, 224-236. Most exegetes agree that this pericope, which is integrated in some manuscript traditions of the gospel of Luke, did not form part of the gospel of John in its original form, but does indeed give an authentic picture of Jesus' praxis.

inscribed in the form of a book, was aimed at the establishment of a God-centred society. With respect to the woman caught in adultery, however, it functioned as a repressive narrative, lacking any openness towards God. By proclaiming, 'Let anyone among you who is without sin be the first to throw a stone at her', Jesus does not annul the law, he simply rids it of its closed logic by pointing to its repressive bias. Jesus thus pushes the Pharisees and the scribes away from the 'addresser' stance of lawmaker and judge, and makes it clear to them that they too are addressees and that the 'addresser' stance itself must remain open. The theme of 'writing in the sand', which commentators see as a reference to Jer 17,13,[3] underlines this: the conduct and way of life (concept of the law) of the religious authorities is not directed towards God. Furthermore, as we can read in verse 6, it is evident that Jesus' pronouncement rids the discourse of the scribes and Pharisees of a second degree of closedness. In questioning Jesus, their primary intention was to trap him into blasphemy, a lack of respect for the divine law. Jesus, moreover, restores the woman's right to speak — a right that was taken from her by the hegemonic discourse of the law — and liberates her from the narrative of sin and guilt in which she had become ensnaed.

From the perspective of the evangelist, Jesus' linguistic act does not indeed result in blasphemy. Jesus reveals who God truly is by acting as God would act: doing justice to this woman. Schnackenburg writes in his commentary on this pericope: "It is not a question of the condemnation of sin but of the appeal to sinners, nor is it a question of the law but of an event. In God's name, Jesus

---

[3] Jer 17,13: 'All who forsake you shall be put to shame; those who turn away from you shall be written *in the earth [in the underworld]*, for they have forsaken the Lord, the fountain of living water' (italics supplied). The term 'written in the earth [in the underworld]' — translated from the Hebrew — is rendered in the LXX as: 'epi tès gès grafètosan'.

takes the side of the sinner; he does not desire to condemn but rather to save."[4]

The gospels frequently employ such verbal altercations as a means to break open closed narratives. Jesus' conversation with the Samaritan woman and the discussion that followed among his disciples immediately springs to mind in this regard (Jn 4,1-42). Not only does Jesus break through the barrier between Jews and Samaritans on two occasions (the second on a matter of principle: true worshippers worship in spirit and truth, vv. 23-24), but he likewise opens the discourse on nourishment and material survival in a dual fashion: water (vv. 13-14, water from the well) and food (vv. 31-34, the disciples bring food from the city and ask him to eat), into a discourse on true life based on spiritual food (living water and food 'that you do not know'). The ultimate result of Jesus' dealings with the Samaritan woman is that the city in which she lives comes to faith. The other evangelists similarly include verbal altercations in which the praxis of the open narrative is given concrete form. In Mk 12,13-17 (and parallels), for instance, the Pharisees and the Herodians try to trap Jesus by asking him whether it is admissible to pay taxes to Caesar: a positive answer from Jesus would have unmasked him as a false messiah while a negative answer would have amounted to a rebellion against the Roman authorities. On this occasion also, Jesus opens up the discourse in a two-fold way: first, the discourse set up by the Pharisees and the scribes in order to trick him, and second, the discourse of 'belonging to', of 'being indebted to'. The statement, 'Give to the emperor the things that belong to the emperor', prepares the way for, 'and to God the things that belong to God': just as the coin bears the image of the emperor and belongs to the emperor, so the human person as image of God (Gen 1,26) belongs to God. By means of

---

[4] R. Schnackenburg, *Das Johannesevangelium*, 232 (our translation).

his reply, Jesus makes a clear distinction between the discourse related to money and the narrative of God in relation to human persons.[5] See also, in this regard, the pericope on the widow's farthing (Mk 12,41-44, parallel Lk 21,1-4) in which a similar distinction between discourses arises. The discourse related to money is given a function in an open narrative directed towards God.[6]

Jesus likewise applies the praxis of the open narrative in his *actions* as well as his words. A candid example of this critical-liberating praxis can be found in the pericope of the purification of the temple, a narrative to be found in all four gospels (Mk 11,15-19, parallel Jn 2,13-25). Jesus drives out the merchants, peddlers and moneychangers from the temple and then admonishes them for making the 'house of prayer' into a 'den of robbers' (Jn: a market). With this bold action he indicts the perversion of the religious open narrative: the temple no longer functions as the place of mediation between God and people. Religion had become linked to the sale of animals for sacrifice and the exchange of money for the temple tax,[7] whereby profit took precedence over prayer.

Such critique of *the reduction of the religious narrative into a closed narrative* takes on a variety of forms in the gospels. We

---

[5] See J. Gnilka, *Das Evangelium nach Markus (Mk. 8,27-16,20),* Evangelisch-katholischer Kommentar zum Neuen Testament, II/2 (Zurich/Neukirchen, 1979), 150-155, pp. 153-54; C.J. den Heyer, *Marcus II. Een praktische bijbelverkla-ring,* Tekst en toelichting (Kampen, 1985) 81: "The second phrase not only relativizes the first, but completely dominates it. God, to whom the entire person belongs, ultimately determines what belongs to Caesar and where the limits of his power lie." See also J.A. Fitzmyer, *The Gospel According to Luke (X-XXIV),* The Anchor Bible, 28a (New York, 1985) 1289-1297, pp. 1293-1294, who in his discussion of the parallel pericope in Luke (Lk 20,20-26) emphasises that the answer of Jesus brings the discussion to a higher level: the relationship between humans and God.

[6] See J. Gnilka, *Das Evangelium nach Markus (Mk. 8,27-16,20),* 177-178.

[7] According to Gnilka, this tax could not be paid with pagan coins. With the exchange, the moneychangers charged a percentage. See *Ibidem,* 126-132, p. 128.

have already mentioned Jesus' critique of the closed narrative of the law and the marketisation of one's relationship with God (which ought in the first place to be one of prayer). We will return in more detail to his piercing critique of the Pharisees and the scribes below. The miracle narratives — a different set of narratives dealing with the performative acts of Jesus — also tell of an event that radically throws open a closed, repressive narrative. In the healing miracles, for example, it is not unusual for physical healing to be related to the forgiveness of sins. In a context in which physical suffering was considered as punishment for a sinful life, this is hardly surprising. Healing is thus a tangible expression of the forgiveness people received for their sins. Mk 2,1-12 presents both discourses together — in their differences and associations — in the story of the healing of the lame man. The phrase, 'Son, your sins are forgiven', is not immediately linked with the command, 'Stand up, take your mat and go to your home', but is followed by a (partly unarticulated) discussion with the scribes. They dispute the authority of Jesus to forgive sins (and thus his critical-liberating praxis of the open narrative), considering his behaviour to be blasphemy, a crime that demanded the death penalty. The healing miracle then follows in order to demonstrate the actuality of Jesus' gift of forgiveness in the name of God. The forgiveness of sins, or alternatively the breaking open of the hegemonic, closed narrative in which people have become ensnared, is given priority.[8] The diversity of these 'ensnaring' narratives is also to be found in other pericopes. In the healing narrative of the ten lepers (Lk 17,11-19), for example, different closed narratives intersect each other: the personal narrative of the sin of the lepers (leprosy was the ultimate punishment

---

[8] See J. Gnilka, *Das Evangelium nach Markus (Mk. 1-8,26)*, Evangelisch-katholischer Kommentar zum Neuen Testament, II/1 (Zurich/Neukirchen, 1978) 95-102, p. 98 ff.

for sin), the narrative of the exclusion of the lepers by the (healthy) community and the narrative of the mutual ostracisation of the Jews and Samaritans which is shattered by the return of the one Samaritan who was healed. Where narratives are opened, God enters into the discussion: the healing results in praise of God — and ultimately, as verse 19b reveals, has everything to do with faith: 'Your faith has made you well.'[9]

A further example is the narrative of Zacchaeus, the chief tax collector of Jericho, which is often seen — perhaps erroneously — as a conversion narrative (Lk 19,1-10). Jesus calls Zacchaeus down from the tree and gives him the chance to speak which had been denied him by his profession (and wealth). (Fitzmyer doubts whether Zacchaeus is portrayed as a sinner in this pericope; the tax collector, he maintains, needs to be seen in contrast to the rich young man of Lk 18 who, although faithful to the law, was unable to part with his wealth). Zacchaeus bears witness to the liberating event of Jesus' word for a social outcast by acting in a liberating way himself. Jesus' closing words have a bearing on the 'event' that overcame Zacchaeus: 'Today salvation has come to this house because he too is a son of Abraham'. At the same time they serve to typify the task Jesus had taken upon himself: 'The Son of Man came to seek and save the lost'. According to Fitzmyer, these words are meant for the bystanders who had prematurely rejected Zacchaeus from their community.[10]

With his resistance to hegemonic closed narratives, which we have been able to illustrate in all the pericopes mentioned so far, and his evident desire to make room for an open narrative in which victims of hegemonic narratives can regain their voice — the praxis of the open narrative — Jesus not only aroused the *amazement* of the

---

[9] See J.A. Fitzmyer, *The Gospel according to Luke*, 1148-1156, pp. 1151-1152.
[10] See *Ibid.*, 1218-1227, pp. 1220-1222.

bystanders, but at the same time he summoned the forces behind the hegemonic narratives against him *in their defence*. Immediately after Jesus drove the moneychangers out of the temple, for instance, Mark describes the surprise and bewilderment of the people *and* the plans of the high priests and scribes to kill him because they were afraid of him (Mk 11,18).

We conclude this illustrative summary of Jesus' critical-liberating praxis of the open narrative by mentioning that many of the pericopes that bear witness to the breaking open of ensnaring and suffocating narratives not only aim at critically unmasking these narratives and making room for their victims, they also constitute *an invitation to us to enter into the praxis of the open narrative*, to follow Jesus. Jesus preached a narrative of conversion that serves also as a call to discipleship. He not only invites outcasts and sinners to enter once again into the life of the community by shattering the hegemonic narrative of the community and its narrowed fidelity to the law, he also creates the conditions whereby the sinner has access to the open narrative. The sinner is thus challenged to transform his or her closed narrative of sin into an open narrative directed towards God. Ultimately, Jesus' activity as a whole is oriented towards the provision of access for all men and women into such an open narrative.

Bearing witness to the Kingdom of God in open narratives

Jesus' activity in word and deed, in line with the praxis of the open narrative, functions simultaneously to 'bear witness'. It reflects a non-dominating, *evocative, witness-bearing* approach to language and to the *inexpressible salvific reality* of God. In his witness to the reign of God, this 'open' character of his discourse becomes even clearer. His preferred way of doing this was to use short stories, literally *open* narratives that we refer to as *parables* or comparisons. 'The kingdom of God is as if someone would scatter seed on the ground' (Mk 4,26); 'like a landowner who went out early in the morning to hire labourers for his vineyard' (Mt 20,1); 'like ten bridesmaids' (Mt 25,1); 'as if a man, going on a journey, summoned his slaves and entrusted his property to them' (Mt 25,14, Lk 19,12); 'The kingdom of heaven may be compared to someone who sowed good seed in his field' (Mt 13,24); '[The kingdom of God] is like a mustard seed' (Mk 4,31 parr.); 'The kingdom of heaven is like yeast' (Mt 13,33a); 'like treasure hidden in a field […], like a merchant in search of fine pearls' (Mt 13,44.45); 'like a net that was thrown into the sea' (Mt 13,47), 'a king who gave a wedding banquet' (Mt 22,2). Mark and Matthew indicate, moreover, that speaking in parables was precisely Jesus' way of conversing with the people (Mk 4,33-34; Mt 13,34-35).[11]

Inspired by Paul Ricoeur, the New Testament exegete Jan Lambrecht notes that a parable sets a metaphorical process in motion that brings about semantic innovation.[12] The person who speaks in parables aims at *the generation of new insights*. As a metaphorical process, a parable should not be explained *by us*; rather it explains *to us* what it stands for. While we pointed out above that Jesus' praxis is intended to stimulate *discipleship*, the parable also invites its hearers' *conversion* and *commitment*. As a word-event, the parable not only bears witness to the event of grace, it also attempts to convey the same grace to the listener who, if he/she is open to it, becomes aware of the interruption of his/her old certainties and is challenged to conversion and commitment.[13] In other words: explicit witness or kerygma calls for praxis.

[11] Gnilka states that Mk 4,34b (Jesus explains the parables to his disciples), which no longer appears in Matthew, fits into Mark's redactional scheme of the messianic secret. Ultimately, the parables for Mark are not understandable without the knowledge of his secret (J. Gnilka, *Das Evangelium nach Markus (Mk. 1-8,26)*, 191).

[12] See, for example, P. Ricoeur, *La métaphore vive* (Paris, 1975).

[13] See J. Lambrecht, *Out of the Treasure. The Parables in the Gospel of Matthew*, Louvain Theological and Pastoral Monographs, 10 (Leuven, 1992) 27-29. See

A salient illustration of this process is provided by the parable of the good Samaritan (Lk 10,25-37). The parable is intended not so much as a revelation of the kingdom of God, but rather as a fitting explanation of the foundational commandment of love. As far as this commandment itself is concerned, it is striking that in Luke the love of God and neighbour (Deut 6,4-5 and Lev 19,18 respectively) are mutually related in the same commandment, while in Mark the commandments are mentioned separately (Mk 12,30-31).[14] A lawyer wants to test Jesus and asks what he must do to gain eternal life. Jesus lets the man himself answer from the Mosaic law: the double commandment of love of God and neighbour. In response to the question, 'Who is my neighbour?', Jesus narrates the parable of the good Samaritan. What is unusual here is the fact that Jesus himself concludes the parable with a question: 'Which of these three [the priest, the Levite, or the Samaritan] proved himself a neighbour to the man who fell into the hands of the robbers?' The passive 'neighbour', the one we are called to love by the commandment of love of neighbour, is inverted by this question (semantically innovated) into the active 'becoming-neighbour' of the one who is addressed by the commandment.[15] The explanation of the commandment of love thus is no longer seen as a theoretical matter, it implies rather a direct claim. The discourse of explanation is thus resolutely broken open. The conviction that mercy towards one's neighbour is salvific is not a merely 'conceptual' matter, it implies that we must actually become neighbour to the other if we are to gain any genuine perspective on 'eternal life' (Lk 10,25b).

also Id., *Terwijl hij tot ons sprak. Parabels van Jezus* (Tielt, [3]1981) 19-22, 28-29, 34-36.

[14] See J. Lambrecht, *Terwijl hij tot ons sprak. Parabels van Jezus*, 86-87: both commandments are "fused into one sentence."

[15] See *Ibid.*, 80: 'Neighbour' shifts from the position of the other as an object of the act to the 'I' as subject of the act.

When the lawyer gives the correct answer to Jesus' question he is told to 'go and do likewise'. Although perhaps incidental to the primary focus of the parable, it is not unimportant to note that a Samaritan (an apostate in the eyes of the Jews) was the one who displayed genuine neighbourliness and not the priest or the Levite. In this way, our attention is drawn to a double interruption of the traditional religious narrative: in the first instance the narrative of the antimony between the Jews and the Samaritans and in the second instance the narrative of the classical Jewish religiosity of the time. It was precisely for deeply religious motivations (fear of becoming ritually impure and thus unable to serve God) that the priest and the Levite refused to help a wounded victim of robbery and violence.

A similar dynamic lies hidden in the parable of Lazarus and the rich man (Lk 16,19-31). The well-to-do and socially-eminent rich man, who has no time for the poor man Lazarus, is ultimately imprisoned in "a futureless isolation, a dream of paradise without the poor."[16] By refusing to recognise Lazarus, the rich man refuses to recognise God and immediately cuts himself off from any association with God (the name Lazarus, incidentally, is based on the expression *El azar* which means 'God helps').

The fact that Jesus' discourse about God and parables over God's kingdom are intended to reveal the profound mystery of a God who *is* love and who *calls us* to love is further illustrated by the parable of the prodigal son (Lk 15,11-32), sometimes referred to by commentators as the parable of the merciful father (or the obedient eldest son). The narrative does not portray God as a stern judge who is unrelenting in his lust for obedience, thus inspiring fear and angst among his followers, but as a loving father who welcomes the return of his youngest son with open arms. It is for this reason that

---

[16] A. Jansen, *Hij sprak tot het volk in parabels*, 112.

the message of the parable is actually intended for those who identify themselves with the eldest son, for those who remain obedient to the father, *in casu* the legally-minded Pharisees. "The Pharisee is without doubt a noble individual: he belongs to the most earnest spiritual movement of the day with an extraordinary religious commitment. As a Pharisee he must avoid any transgression of the law, whatever the cost, but he does so with military obedience. While he is always correct, his correctness is inspired by fear. He maintains the customary image of a father as an authoritative guarantor of law and order. In the parable's plot, he is suddenly confronted with the possibility that another father exists, a father characterised by intense goodness, incredible compassion and unending solicitude. This is a decisive discovery which Jesus himself had also experienced: God is different, God *is love* (1 Jn 4,8)."[17]

Jesus' open Abba-relationship as basic attitude

Jesus' indictment of closed narratives and his witness to the God of love have their roots in his *fundamental contemplative attitude,* an openness towards the Other who is revealed in moments of interruption. Such an open attitude is characteristic of *an authentic relationship with God and one's fellow humans,* articulated in the aforementioned double commandment: 'Love God above all and your neighbour as yourself' (Mk 12,28-34 parr.). Shortly after this double commandment, we read in both Mark and Matthew — in their accusations against the scribes and Pharisees (Mk 12,37b-40 parr.) — that a non-authentic relationship with God is precisely due to a lack of a contemplative openness.[18] Matthew develops the

---

[17] L. Aerts, "De bijbel: het verhaal blijft open," *TGL* 52 (1996) 143-157, p. 151.

[18] See J. Gnilka, *Das Matthäusevangelium. II. Teil,* Herder Theologischer Kommentar zum Neuen Testament (Freiburg/Basel/Vienna, ²1992) 270-295.

indictment against these religious authorities in a detailed way (Mt 23,1-12) and adds in addition a further seven 'woe sayings' against them (Mt 23,13-36). As religious authorities it is claimed that while they set themselves up as 'masters' of the religious narrative (v. 2: they sit on the chair of Moses), they forget that in the first place they themselves are addressees of the narrative. Moreover, they pervert the religious narrative because their words and deeds are not directed towards God, but are aimed solely at the acquisition of fame, recognition and privileged treatment (vv. 5-6: broad phylacteries, places of honour at feasts and the best seats in the synagogue). The fact that they let themselves be called rabbi, father and leader, while there is but one rabbi, one Father, one Lord (vv. 7-10), testifies to these two reproaches. The text states how things should in fact be: 'The greatest among you shall be your servant'(v. 11). The woe sayings continue to cut to the core of their perversion of religion. The scribes and the Pharisees are angrily accused because — in their rigorous fidelity to the law — they disregard what the law and religion are all about: justice, mercy and faithfulness (v. 23, in Lk 11,42: justice and the love of God), three relational attitudes which give the fulfilment of the law its proper place in the religious narrative that stands open towards God. The woe sayings conclude with the reproach that the scribes and the Pharisees have murdered those who bear witness to religion as an open narrative, namely the prophets (and Jesus himself whom they are planning to murder). Their closed narrative leads to death and creates victims. It will ultimately turn against them.[19]

The fundamental contemplative attitude is also evoked positively in the Sermon on the Mount in Matthew (Mt 5,2-7,27),[20] in which

---

[19] See the second quotation in the superscript to part three.

[20] See Id., *Das Matthäusevangelium. I. Teil,* Herder Theologischer Kommentar zum Neuen Testament (Freiburg/Basel/Vienna, 1986) 111 ff.

it acquires the connotations of radical love (5,43-48), authenticity in giving alms and in prayer (6,1-4.5-6[.7-13]), readiness to forgive (6,14-15), attention to more than just the material (6,19-21) and full surrender to this option for 'more' (for no one can serve two masters, 6,24), freedom from care (like the birds of the air and the lilies of the field, 6,25-34), suspension of one's own judgement (7,1-5), trust in God (7,7-11). In addition, given that the call of the first disciples is placed immediately before the Sermon on the Mount (Mt 4,18-22), one can add complete availability to this series of connotations (this is also apparent in Mt 8,18). To become like children (Mt 18,1-5 parr.), and finally to be vulnerable, to be open to persecution (Mk 13,9-13 parr.), conclude the series. The fact that such a fundamental contemplative attitude is not acquired without a fight but is tested severely, is testified to by the threefold trial Jesus had to undergo in the desert: the temptation to self-preservation, prestige, possessions and power. Jesus' answers to the devil's question make it clear that all such temptations are rooted in a perverted attitude towards God (Mt 4,1-11, Lk 4,1-13).

According to Edward Schillebeeckx, Jesus of Nazareth's fundamental contemplative attitude is based on his 'Abba-experience'. Jesus' experience of God as Abba also immediately implies, Schillebeeckx notes, an awareness of the obligation to 'do God's will'.[21]

Being open towards God makes Jesus highly sensitive to situations in which this openness is already extensively filled in, closed from the start. The person who maintains an openness for the event of interruption is not only *vulnerable* — in the double sense of the word: sensitive yet open to injury — he/she also recognises where hegemonic narratives eliminate other narratives. In the victims'

---

[21] See E. Schillebeeckx, *Jesus: An Experiment in Christology* (New York, 1981) 256-268.

very incapacity to speak, to have their say, something of the event of the o/Other becomes — negatively — visible. This attention for what is not brought to speech, for the people pushed aside by hegemonic narratives, appears on different occasions in Jesus' words and deeds. Here also we witness the application of Jesus' critical-liberating activity, the salvation of what has been lost. Salvation is promised to the one who opens him/herself and acts accordingly as well as the one who endures injury (Mt 5,1-12).

3. THE JESUS-NARRATIVE: THE COMPLETION AND THE PROMISE OF THE OPEN NARRATIVE

The evangelists make Jesus known as someone who speaks and acts according to the praxis of the open narrative. At a deeper level also, however, the open narrative structure is present in a meaningful way: the Jesus-narrative itself lies before us as an open narrative. According to the witness of the New Testament, it is a narrative of someone who, precisely due to his lived praxis, is pushed aside by the religious and political authorities and definitively deprived of his say, only to have it restored to him by God. Where the hegemonic narrative of the elders and the scribes destroyed Jesus, God offers a future. "The good news of the resurrection lies herein, that it destroys the unyielding law of fate that Jesus would be condemned to suffering and death. It implies a breach with this fate that would have made of Jesus' life a failure."[22]

The experience of this breach, i.e., the shattering of the hegemonic narrative of rejection and death, has become, in the meantime,

---

[22] T. Radcliffe, "Theologie als repeterende breuk. Het Nieuwe Testament en de Dag van Vandaag," ed. E. Schillebeeckx a.o., *Breuklijnen. Grenservaringen en zoektochten* (Fs. T. Schoof) (Baarn, 1994) 67-80, p. 67. Radcliffe continues: "Christian theology is always a proclamation of this breach."

the faith experience of the disciples.[23] This Jesus who died on the cross is alive: an experience felt by the disciples to be salvific for their own life stories as well. This Jesus continues his involvement with them and brings salvation to those who believe in him. Schillebeeckx speaks in this regard of a conversion experience, i.e., "the experience of having received forgiveness from Jesus — a quite specific experience of grace and mercy, the result of which was that they were received back into a present fellowship with Jesus and confessed him to be their definitive salvation, which was not at an end with his death and through which they were brought together again and restored to fellowship with him and each other."[24]

This is the *key event* to which the Christian open narrative testifies. It is not for nothing that a collection of narratives and words on the passion and resurrection event of Jesus would first serve as the foundation of the now familiar gospels and only later be supplemented with additional material. In Jesus himself the open narrative is completed in such a way that it becomes a *promise* for the disciples. They begin to confess the crucified and risen One as the One who is to come: in the event of the resurrection they experience a renewed offer of salvation.[25]

The question, '*What does Jesus do?*', is thus associated with the question, '*Who is Jesus?*'. Rooted in their experience of the resurrection — God's active intervention in the narrative of Jesus — the first disciples not only preach the message of Jesus as saviour, they also preach the person of Jesus. For Christians, belief in the gospels

---

[23] For the paragraphs below, see: E. Schillebeeckx, *Jesus*, 379ff.

[24] *Ibid.*, 381-382. In his dissection of the appearance narratives, Schillebeeckx insists that we are dealing with an experience of conversion. They are referring in essence to a grace experience, the "experience of new being that imparts to faith the assurance that Jesus is alive" (p. 392).

[25] See *Ibid.*, 390.

(= the good news) does not only mean belief in Jesus' message but also belief in Jesus himself as the revelation of God. God makes Godself known in the very words, deeds and person of Jesus as the God of love. It is for this reason that the first Christians testified to Jesus as the Messiah, as the Son of God, as the Son of Man, etc. In other words, Jesus is not only the interrupter of closed narratives, he is also an inviting event for men and women of all times. For those who believe, Jesus' words and deeds are from God and they serve simultaneously as the revelation of a God who is concerned with the well-being of humanity.

4. TALKING ABOUT JESUS IN OPEN NARRATIVES

Of course our reasoning up to this point has been unavoidably determined by the fact that the gospels themselves already bear witness to Jesus of Nazareth who, after the Easter event, is identified with the risen Christ. On the level of the gospel, the evangelist bears witness to Jesus much more than describing his day-to-day existence. After the Easter experience, it is apparently only possible for the early church to speak of the Jesus-narrative in the mode of the open narrative, indeed *as* an open narrative. The result is a Christian open narrative of the open narrative revealed and lived in Christ. We briefly outline the implications of this below.

Parables about Jesus

The new insight introduced by the resurrection into the life of the disciples concerning the person of Jesus of Nazareth inspired them to bear witness to the same Jesus. Parables told by Jesus as illustrations of the kingdom of God thus became vehicles intended to bear witness to Jesus himself. The parables in which Jesus spoke about God and God's will for humanity and the world were recontextualised as it were. As with the kingdom of God, the post-Easter Jesus can only be described in evocative and imaginative terminology.

The first Christians related some of the parables to Jesus himself. In the parable of the wicked tenants (Mk 12,1-12 parr.), for example, the owner of the vineyard sends various servants to the tenants to collect his share of the produce. The tenants, however, refuse to hand over the owner's share and they abuse his servants time and again. The owner finally sends his own son, convinced that they will listen to him. Reasoning that the death of the owner's heir will result in their own inheritance of the vineyard, the wicked tenants seize and kill him and throw him out of the vineyard. For the first Christians, the servants sent by the owner represent the many prophets sent by God to his people, while the son represents Jesus Christ. The same Jesus Christ likewise features in the parable of the wise and foolish bridesmaids (Mt 25,1-13). Similarly, Jesus Christ is presented as the final arbiter in Matthew's description of the last judgement. The saved are those who lovingly cared for 'the least of my brothers' (giving food to the hungry, drink to the thirsty, hospitality to the stranger, clothes to the naked, visiting the sick and those in prison). Jesus concludes, 'Truly I tell you, just as you did it to one of the least of these who are members of my family, you did it to me' (Mt 25,40). It is precisely in the face of the other, the face of the victims, that Jesus reveals himself as the Other. From the perspective of the Risen One, the fundamental open attitude is profoundly characterised by sensitivity towards the poor, the weak and the rejected.

Some other elements

A multitude of elements in the gospels — in terms of form and content, language and redaction — serve to underline *the open narrative character of the New Testament witness*. By way of illustration we will examine four such elements. It is evident, for instance, that the writer of the oldest gospel, Mark, ends his gospel in an 'open' way with the women who, out of consternation and fear, ran away from the tomb and said nothing to anyone (Mk 16,8). Rooted in fear, this 'silence' closes the tomb pericope *and* the gospel. According to J. Gnilka, this is of the utmost theological importance for Mark: Mark is aware that his mediation of the faith can only serve as a guide, can only lead people to the boundaries of becoming a believer. Only in discipleship, in the praxis of the open narrative, is it possible to witness further to what 'happens' in faith. The full understanding of the 'open' Jesus-narrative is to be found beyond Mk 16,8.[26] The fact that this open conclusion came as something of a surprise and ultimately implied a serious injunction for its readers/audience, was picked up quite quickly and was apparently difficult to maintain in its full demanding power. In the history of the transmission of the manuscripts, diverse attempts have been undertaken to give the gospel a 'real' conclusion.[27]

A further peculiarity evident in Mark is the so-called messianic secret. J. Lambrecht maintains that this secret is an invention of Mark who was concerned "about the quality of the faith of his [contemporary] fellow men and women, about the purity of their perspective on Christ, their Christology."[28] The disciples' lack of comprehension, which always follows a prediction of Jesus' suffering — in Mk 8,33 on the necessity that the messiah must suffer and in Mk 9,33-34/10,35-37 on the status of disciples in the coming kingdom — stands as a model for the lack of comprehension

---

[26] See J. Gnilka, *Das Evangelium nach Markus (Mk. 8,27-16,20)*, 344-345.

[27] For a basis for this paragraph, see *Ibid.*, pp. 350-351. Besides the longer, canonical conclusion (Mk 16,9-20) Gnilka then also includes the so-called shorter conclusion in his commentary (pp. 351-358).

[28] J. Lambrecht, *Hij gaat voor ons uit. Jezus volgen in het marcusevangelie* (Leuven, [3]1985) 20. See further also: ed. C. Tuckett, *The Messianic Secret*, Issues in Religion and Theology, 1 (Philadelphia/London, 1983) (with a bibliography).

of all those who impatiently desire to interpret Jesus-as-Messiah and the reign of God, the lack of comprehension of all those who want to close the painful openness of the Christian narrative out of misunderstanding or a concern for self-preservation.[29] The transfiguration narrative (Mk 9,2-10 parr.) serves as a further illustration. On a high mountain and in the presence of three of his disciples, Jesus is transfigured and enters into conversation with Moses and Elijah after which a voice coming from a cloud that had overshadowed them proclaims: 'This is my Son, the Beloved; listen to him!' (Mk 9,7). Luke writes that the external appearance of his face became different (Lk 9,29). Moreover, his clothes became so white 'such as no one on earth could bleach them' (Mk 9,3). The glorified Christ cannot be grasped in his earthly form. When Peter, filled with awe, proposes that three tents be built, it is clear indeed that he is lost for words (Mk 9,6). The evangelist, who resorts to using this narrative to express something about Jesus, then lets God himself typify Jesus, after which he suddenly concludes the event: when they looked around, they saw no one anymore except Jesus and themselves.

The fact that the risen Christ is not to be grasped in his earthly form — although, at the same time, inseparable from his earthly form — is expressed in an exceptional way by the narrative of the disciples on the road to Emmaus (Lk 24,13-32). The two travellers to Emmaus meet a stranger who, in the course of the encounter, reveals himself in word and deed[30] to be the Christ. Upon recognition, however, he immediately withdraws from them.

---

[29] Concerning the disciples and their (our) difficulty in grasping Jesus' message, see also: G. Van Oyen, "'Bekeer U en geloof in de blijde boodschap'. Verandering in het Marcusevangelie," ed. L. Boeve, *De kerk in Vlaanderen,* 126-145.

[30] Words and deeds that in reference to the scriptures — beginning with Moses — recontextualisingly explain the complete Jesus-narrative.

Plurality as medium of the open narrative and as its result

The somewhat randomly selected scriptural examples discussed above reflect an initial impression, one to which the history of the Jesus narrative — and indeed the very formation of what we call the New Testament — continued to testify. This impression must have been present from very early on. It is remarkable indeed that the New Testament speaks of the person of Jesus Christ, as well as the grace experienced in his person, by means of a plurality of titles and models, which are associated with Jesus Christ himself and the grace experienced in him. One has a sense that even at this early stage it was difficult to express precisely what one wanted to express about Jesus. Such titles include: Lord, Christ/Messiah, Son of Man, Son of David, Prophet, Son, Son of God, Word. The confessional context within which these titles appear further underlines their witness character.[31] The variety of expressions employed for the grace experienced in Jesus Christ includes: the experience of being a child of God, of having received the spirit, of having become Christ-like (through discipleship); and more concretely: the experience of wholeness and salvation, being wrenched away from slavery and subjugation, liberation by means of ransom, reconciliation after strife, redemption as atonement, redemption as expiation of sins, redemption as the forgiveness of sins, redemption towards community, towards brotherly love, towards freedom, fullness of life, and so on.[32]

---

[31] Schillebeeckx (*Jesus*, 403-436), for instance, enumerates four types of early-Christian creeds in which christological titles appear with a changing and at times very paradoxical content: *maranatha*-christology (Jesus, the one who brings the salvation that is to come, the Lord of the future and the judge of the world*)*, *theos-anèr*-christology (Jesus, the divine miracle worker), wisdom christologies (Jesus, the messenger of Wisdom and the wisdom teacher; Jesus, the pre-existing, incarnated, humiliated but also glorified wisdom); and Easter-christologies (Jesus, the Crucified and Risen one).

[32] See Id., *Christ: The Experience of Jesus as Lord* (New York, 1989).

We encounter a similar plurality on the level of the gospels themselves. The young Church apparently deemed it necessary to accept four gospels as canonical, all of which contradict each other on some points. Each of these gospels, moreover, displays a different image of Jesus and is characterised by a specific contextual and theological perspective — so much so that one can speak of a Matthean, Markan, Lukan and Johannine theology. Evidently, the young churches did not take such contradiction and diversity to be disruptive. What lay at the foundation of the decision to recognise the four gospels as canonical was the insight that it was impossible to grasp the truth about Jesus Christ unmediated, and that this truth could only be evoked via a plurality of images and narratives.[33] Furthermore, attempts, such as that of Tatianus, to construct *one* harmonious gospel out of the four gospels, or selectively maintain only *one* gospel as canonical, as in the case of Marcion who rejected the canonicity of Matthew, Mark and John, remained unsuccessful.[34]

Finally, the existence, side-by-side, of four canonical gospels is not alone in witnessing to the open structure of the early Church's testimony to the Christian faith. The same can be said of the various genres present in the New Testament as a whole, which came into existence in a variety of well-determined historical contexts. The form of the witness evidently changed according to the changing

[33] Radcliffe also describes the canon as a symbolisation of the church that, in its plurality of traditions, felt itself one in Christ: "The canon was the symbol of the incessant dialogue between the churches, one and many, united in a faith that surpasses every separate theological perspective" (T. Radcliffe, *Theologie als repeterende breuk*, 75). For this paragraph, see also: D. Tracy, "Reading the Bible," Id., *On Naming the Present. Reflections on God, Hermeneutics and the Church* (Maryknoll, 1994) 120-130.

[34] Be that as it may, the official diversity recognised by the Church is recontextualised at least today in this manner — a manner that is supported by the remark in the following paragraph.

demands of the context. As we noted above, Jesus employed parables to evoke the kingdom of God. A further form of witness emerged when the Christian faith spread out around the Mediterranean and the way in which communities tended to form around Jesus effectively changed. Such a diaspora of small communities required a 'new theological medium': the writing of letters. This method lost some of its binding force when the first generation of believers died and when the communities were pressured by persecutions: Christians betrayed their fellow Christians (Mk 13,12-13). The negative effects of failure and betrayal opened a new perspective on what it might mean to be one with Christ and demonstrated the importance of a new, radicalised appropriation of the Christian identity. The genre of the gospel complied precisely with this new context. Mark recounted the narrative of Jesus in such a way that it was long enough to draw in the reader. Starting from the experience of failure, it teaches that there is a way out of failure for Christians: "The tomb is empty and they have to go to Galilee where they will see him."[35]

In short: as the context changed in the New Testament communities, the Christian message acquired a different appearance. Continuity thus takes shape in rupture. Indeed this process of continuity continues to the present day thanks only to such ruptures. Every age is in search of a new and appropriate form with which it can continue to recount the open narrative of Jesus Christ to future generations.[36]

5. A TWO-PART CONCLUSION

At the opening of this chapter we posed two questions: (i) Is it possible on theological grounds to speak of the Christian narrative as an

---

[35] T. Radcliffe, *Theologie als repeterende breuk*, 74.
[36] In this perspective, the history of religious art for instance could be re-narrated.

'open narrative'? (ii) What would the theological consequences of such an endeavour be? We responded to the first question with an explicit affirmation. The structure of the model of the open narrative is not only recognisable for those who read the foundational source texts, it also enjoys Christological motivation. The theological consequences of this affirmation are far-reaching. In the process of recontextualisation we undertook with the aid of the critical consciousness as developed in the model of the open narrative, we discovered the Christian narrative as a very specific open narrative, marked by a critical-liberative praxis, the testimony to an interrupting God, and the nourishing of a contemplative open attitude. In confrontation with contemporary critical consciousness, the Christian narrative recognises productive patterns whereby it can unfold its own internal rationale in a plausible manner and continue to challenge Christians to hazard the engagement of conversion and discipleship.

Jesus: paradigm of the open narrative

In his life and person, Jesus is recognised as a normative witness to the open narrative. In word and deed he facilitated access to the interruptive event of grace, challenged all to abandon their closed narratives and to enter into an open narrative directed towards God. After the resurrection event the risen Jesus is recognised as grace, as the one who opens the closed narratives in a liberative way.[37]

---

[37] Compare R.G. Cote, "Ambiguity as Invitation to Believe," *Kerygma* 24 (1990) 181-192: Cote pleads for a theology of ambiguity, proceeding from the ambiguity that Jesus both created and underwent creation, and which displays a notable affinity with the theology of the open narrative that we have developed. Synthesizing both positions from the perspective of our own, we could state that ambiguity is an enduring characteristic of one who narrates an open narrative because this, in pointing away from one's own narrative to the inexpressible in order to thus evoke it, can never (and in principle) obtain the clarity and unequivocality of a closed description.

Indeed, the New Testament writers and, as we noted above, the evangelists in particular, endeavoured in their words about Jesus to highlight the challenging significance he had for them. They bore witness to being captured by Jesus Christ and to the salvation they experienced in him, and they invited their contemporaries to follow in his footsteps, to enter into his open narrative. They in turn attempted, in their own way, in their witness, to facilitate access to the interruptive event.

Paul's letters precede the efforts of the evangelists. In his letter to the Galatians, he bears witness to the grace that overcame him (Gal 2,15-21). He writes that in his encounter with the risen one, he came to the insight that the works of the law did not justify him and that only faith in Jesus Christ led to true justification. At the same time, he claims that he was gifted in this graced encounter with the possibility of becoming part of this faith. Paul describes precisely this experience as a personal resurrection event: he is crucified with Christ and is risen with him, so much so that he can even state: 'It is no longer I who live, but it is Christ who lives in me' (Gal 2,20a). From this point on he denounces the law, the yoke of slavery that is broken by the coming of Christ.[38] It is not by fulfilling the law that one assures one's salvation; salvation is only possible in being open for Christ. This is the truth of the gospel (Gal 2,5.14). 'You who want to be justified by the law have cut yourselves off from Christ; you have fallen away from grace' (Gal 5,4). It is this very openness for Christ, or put differently, the life in the Spirit, which is Christian, graced freedom: not as one disjoined from the law in the negative sense of the word, nor as a licence for

---

[38] It is probable that the opponents of Paul, after his missionary work in Galatia, taught that the observation of the law and the rite of circumcision were necessary requirements in order to enter into the Christian community. See H.D. Betz, *Galatians. A Commentary on Paul's Letter to the Churches in Galatia,* Hermeneia - A Critical and Historical Commentary on the Bible (Philadelphia, 1979) 7.

'self-centred egotism', but as a positive freedom to love one another. We prefer to speak of this freedom as the possibility of entering into the praxis of the open narrative. The fruits of such a praxis are the fruits of the Spirit: 'love, joy, peace, patience, kindness, generosity, faithfulness, gentleness, self-control' (Gal 5,22b).[39] The gospel is not to be identified with the closed narrative of the law, nor with that of 'self-centred egotism', but with the open narrative of love for God and neighbour.

'Imitatio Christi' – discipleship through the praxis of the open narrative

Christianity has the potential to be an open narrative because the image of Jesus, which stems from its earliest sources, allows us to encounter him as the *revelation of God's open narrative*. It is for this reason that we can describe Jesus as *God's interrupter*. This image allows us to see what Jesus does, what he stands for and who he is in a contextually conceivable manner. This opens up the way for Christians to envisage for themselves the experience of salvation in Jesus Christ to which the early disciples bore witness. Such an image, moreover, respects the evocative, inspirational and motivational power of the message and person of Jesus Christ. It contains a compelling invitation to enter into the praxis of the open Christian narrative. This implies, in the first instance, an openness for the unexpected, the other who approaches us — often in concrete form (the poor, the rejected) — and questions our own narrative; secondly, an examination of our own narrative in order

---

[39] In the conclusion of his letter Paul still adds this warning: 'Do not be deceived; God is not mocked, for whatever a man sows, that he will also reap. For he who sows to his own flesh will from the flesh reap corruption; but he who sows to the Spirit will from the Spirit reap eternal life. And let us not grow weary in well doing, for in due season we shall reap, if we do not lose heart' (Gal 6,7-9).

to determine whether the 'other' features therein as one rejected, as one lacking respect; thirdly, a testimony to the fact that in the very confrontation with interruptive otherness, God's grace is at work: interruption opens a pathway to the God of Love, the wholly Other.

This concludes our reflection on the possibility of an 'open Christian narrative'. We have endeavoured to show that the Christian narrative, in terms of both its structure and content, has the potential to recontextualise itself as an open narrative. Indeed, if it wishes to remain faithful to itself in our present day and age, such recontextualisation is imperative. In the following chapter we will discuss the consequences of our movement towards recontextualisation for the way we think and speak about God.

VIII. NEGATIVE THEOLOGY: GOD'S INTERRUPTION OF CHRISTIAN MASTER NARRATIVES

'It is a little past midnight on July 25*th*, 1996, and I am sitting around the table with seven young men and women. The conversation has flagged somewhat. The flickering candles seem to be the only things worthy of our attention. In the intense silence each of us is busy with our own thoughts and the time ticks slowly and irreversibly by. It is the final evening of a week long vacation camp in the German-speaking part of Belgium during which we, as camp leaders, have given our best to a group of sixty ten-year-olds and indeed to one another. During the seven days, which were now drawing to a close, there had been a good atmosphere among the group leaders. The support of the group had allowed each of us to be ourselves, to share our weaknesses and vulnerability and to be listened to with respect. It had been a time of growth for each of us and for the group as a whole, a time that would come to an end on the following day at noon. After forty minutes of what had become unbearable stillness I gathered up the courage to break the silence. Slowly we cleared the table and headed towards our bedrooms. As I left the room, one of the other leaders shared his impressions of the situation, and said, "It is as if we are sitting on top of a mountain and no longer want to descend the slopes and return to base camp." I immediately thought of the transfiguration narrative — 'Let us build three tents in this place' (Mk 9,2-10 and parr.). Many a catechist and youth minister would have grasped the opportunity to draw associations with the Christian faith as an explanatory frame of reference, but on the night of July 25*th* [1996] this would have been far from appropriate. A discussion about God *would simply have been too much, a well-intentioned but scarcely appreciated attempt at recuperation. The interruptive character of the moment had already seen to that. The paradoxical experience of healing and woundedness, of the chance to go home and the obligation to leave, was not open to extrinsic explanation, however evident such an explanation might have been. Perhaps later...'[1]*

On August 22nd, 1996, Liège Cathedral is full to capacity. Two small white coffins are the focus of attention. They contain the last remains of Julie and Melissa, two young girls who had been kidnapped months before, locked up in a cellar, repeatedly abused and left to die from hunger and deprivation. During his homily, the priest, Father Schoonbroodt, asked the painful question which could not have been far from the minds of the disconsolate parents and the rest of the crowd: 'God, where were you?'

1. THE END OF THE CHRISTIAN MASTER NARRATIVE

Both of the illustrations reported above serve as positive and negative experiences of alterity that interrupt our ongoing narratives and force them to their limits. Both moments of interruption remind us in the first place of the fact that experiences of alterity are not necessarily Christian experiences of transcendence. This is only the case when such experiences are rooted in some form of Christian frame of reference that, given the growing tension between faith and culture in our actual plural context, is no longer to be presumed. For *contextual* reasons, an open Christian narrative must be sensitive to this fact: people no longer share the same frame of reference.

Such experiences of alterity, however, have more to say than this. At moments like this the Christian narrative is forced to its

[1] From a leader of a youth movement, Summer 1996.

limits. Within the Christian frame of reference itself, both experiences provoke an interruption of the narrative: language runs aground, we are at a loss for words, our efforts to understand fail us, the experience overwhelms us and shocks us out of our familiar assumptions. Under pressure from such experiences of the otherness of God and God's salvation, the Christian narrative is forced *from within* to structure itself as an open narrative.

The Christian master narrative is no more: every narrative of control confronts us with the uncontrollable. The unassailable other forces us time and again to the limits of every narrative of domination.

2. THE OTHER SIDE: THE REDISCOVERY OF NEGATIVE THEOLOGY

In order to give expression to this sensitivity towards the irreducible other, a number of postmodern philosophers have devoted an increased amount of attention in recent years to the ancient Christian tradition of *negative* or *apophatic* theology.

The name that comes most readily to mind in association with the earliest articulations of this tradition is *(Pseudo-) Dionysius the Aeropagite*,[2] a mystic theologian from the 5th-6th centuries who employed the pseudonym of an Athenian disciple of Paul (Acts 7,34). He maintained that when we speak about God, negations contain more truth than affirmations. It may be correct to affirm that God is 'light' or God is 'king' but, in the last analysis, it is more correct to deny both affirmations. After all, 'light' and 'king' are concepts that cannot precisely render the essence of God. Furthermore, God is beyond all affirmation and negation. In principle, there is nothing we can say about him. Our images, metaphors and

---

[2] Apophatic theological accents were also evident among other Church Fathers, especially Gregory of Nyssa. Figures such as Thomas Aquinas, Meister Eckhart and Nicolas of Cusa were also at home in this tradition.

concepts of God are all ultimately inappropriate, even when they stem from biblical sources. Our knowledge of God is always inadequate. Whenever we try to affirm or negate something about God, we are always short of our target: God rises above our words, is indefinable, incomprehensible to our language and thought.[3] For Dionysius this is not just some kind of word game. For him the dynamic of affirmation and negation is caught up in a mystical movement towards God.

Jacques Derrida explicitly affirms associations between his deconstructionism and the tradition of apophatic theology.[4] He points out, for example, that in the very act of negating God one actually negates one's negation of God. Derrida calls this a *dé-négation*: the most negative discourse always contains a trace of the other. Negation cannot hide or conceal — on the contrary it reveals — the fact that there is always an alterity that precedes speech and makes it possible. We are not at the source of things, we do not have access to this source and we are not its master. In his various writings, Jean-François Lyotard struggled with the task he had taken upon himself to represent the un-representable in its un-representability, to *evoke the inexpressible in its inexpressibility*.[5] For Lyotard, our postmodern sensitivity consists of the awareness that everything we say and everything we represent is accompanied and surrounded

---

[3] See Dionysius Areopagita, "The Mystical Theology," Id., *The Complete Works*, transl. C. Luibheid (New York, 1987) 133-141.

[4] See J. Derrida, "Comment ne pas parler? Dénégations," Id., *Psychè: Inventions de l'autre* (Paris, 1987) 535-595. For a further elaboration and some comments, see L. Boeve, "The Rediscovery of Negative Theology Today: The Narrow Gulf between Theology and Philosophy," Biblioteca dell' *Archivio di filosofia* 29 (2002) 443-460.

[5] J.-F. Lyotard, *Le différend* (Paris, 1983); *Le postmoderne expliqué aux enfants: Correspondance 1982-1985* (Paris, 1986); *L'inhumain: Causeries sur le temps* (Paris, 1988).

by that which remains inexpressible, un-representable. While the inexpressible and the un-representable not only constitute the grounds for the very possibility of speech, they also constitute its most profound obstacle: every pretension to exhaustivity, every claim to be foundational or determinative is thus unmasked. The inexpressible breaks into every discourse as an 'event'. It is precisely this that the so-called master narratives tended to (wanted to) forget and it is this neglect that made them hegemonic.

The interest of these philosophers in negative theology is essentially unrelated to any mystical orientation towards God based on the Christian narrative. They are more concerned about the structural similarities between the tradition of negative theology and their own efforts to discuss the otherness illuminated by the interruptive event. They envisage a way of speaking that, paradoxically enough, is capable of allowing discourse on that which language cannot contain, whereby every linguistic reference is immediately stripped of any potential claim on the subject of the discourse.

In their studies of negative theology, however, such philosophers not only do themselves a service, they also serve contemporary *theologians*, inspiring them to *rediscover a part of their own tradition* and to (re)read the authors who represent that tradition. Theologians can learn from this rediscovery in two ways.

On the one hand, theologians are instructed that negative theology in the apophatic tradition is not only a supplement to positive theology, a sort of complementary relativisation, but rather *the ongoing and requisite background* of every positive statement about God. Down through the centuries, the critical power of negative theology has been all too easily suppressed by its integration in the so-called (neo-) scholastic *tres viae*. In an affirmative statement, something is confirmed about God: e.g. 'God is good'. In the negation thereof, however, the affirmation is then denied: 'God is not good (in the way we as human beings understand and experience goodness)'. The affirmation is then repeated in its most exalted form: 'God is eminently good'. In this threefold method, negation is reduced to a logical step, a rather harmless supplement to a highly affirmative positive theology. The rediscovery of negative theology tends to set aside such conceptualisations and teaches us that this theological method is not so much a way of theologising side by side with — or subordinate to — positive theology. On the contrary, it consists more of an apophatic theological attitude or fundamental position, which carries within it the insight that every theology must admit its basic incapacity to reach God with words and concepts.

On the other hand, many theologians are aware that the very affinity of apophatic theology with present-day sensitivities offers *a new opportunity to engage in the theological endeavour in the actual postmodern context*. Three potential experiences would appear to occasion such an awareness. We will discuss each in turn.

3. THREEFOLD NEGATIVE THEOLOGY

In the following paragraphs we will discuss, in turn, the opportunities for an apophatic theological approach in the realisation of God's incomprehensibility rooted in the experience of God as excessive love; in the realisation of the mystery of God in suffering and conflict; in the experience of God's absence, or rather in the absence of the experience of God.

The incomprehensible God

In our postmodern context, the theological cultivation of negative theology enjoys, in the first instance, the potential to draw associations with postmodern sensitivity towards the other, which in theological terms is a sensitivity towards the Other. In the event of grace, God as Other presents Godself in God's *incomprehensible fullness*, as p*ossibility* and *boundary* of every statement about God. In a number of interrelated essays and articles, the American theologian David Tracy makes a strong case for such postmodern, mystical theologising.[6]

For Tracy, this theology lies somewhere between our awareness of transgression, excess, rupture and invasion, on the one hand, and speechlessness or the incapacity to express this awareness, on the other. Both aspects are related to forms of mysticism found in the Christian tradition: the mysticism of love and apophatic mysticism.[7] The mysticism of love, Tracy notes, exercises an almost irresistible power of attraction on postmodern philosophers such as Bataille, Lacan, Kristeva and Irigaray. Their studies are replete with references to Christian mystics of love such as Bernard of Clairvaux and Theresa of Avila and the excess of love and joy to which they testify in their writings. Continuing this line of approach, Tracy concludes that, in the postmodern theological endeavour, 'God is love' is no longer understood in modern terms as relationship (e.g., between partners) or in premodern terms as emanation (the power of being which emanates from God and fills creation). "Postmoderns make two characteristic moves: either explode or transgress the form of love — beyond modern notions of love as

---

[6] D. Tracy, *On Naming the Present. Reflections on God, Hermeneutics, and Church* (Maryknoll, 1994); see further also Id., "The Hermeneutics of Naming God," *Irish Theological Quarterly* 57 (1991) 253-264; "Literary Theory and Return of the Forms for Naming and Thinking God in Theology," *The Journal of Religion* 74 (1994) 302-319; "Theology and the Many Faces of Postmodernity," *Theology Today* 51 (1994) 104-114.

[7] Tracy refers in this regard to B. McGinn, *The Presence of God: A History of Western Christian Mysticism. I. The Foundations of Western Mysticism* (New York, 1991). McGinn makes a distinction between four types of mysticism: image mysticism, Trinitarian mysticism, love mysticism and apophatic mysticism.

relationality (e.g., process theism and Hegel) and beyond premodern forms of love as overflow and emanation (neoplatonic) into love now understood as sheer excess and transgression."[8] The form of love dissolves into pure formlessness, elusiveness. It is this latter aspect that brings postmodern (philosophers and) theologians together in their interest in the apophatic tradition as it can be found in the work of Pseudo-Dionysius, Scotus Eriugena and Meister Eckhart.

It is striking, moreover, that the negative is no longer associated existentially with the dark night of the modern man and woman who is desperately in search of meaning. God's very incomprehensibility is now valued as a positive element. The radical incomprehensibility of God is cherished as the most adequate way to approach the reality of God as mystery. Postmodern mystical theologians are drawn to this insight, not only because it helps to highlight the boundaries of the human understanding of God, but primarily because it supports their efforts to think about God as God and to speak about God as God rooted in God's radical incomprehensibility.[9]

---

[8] Tracy, "Literary Theory and Return of the Forms for Naming and Thinking God in Theology," 314.

[9] For Tracy this would appear to be the best way to resist the ontotheological temptation introduced by anti-ontotheological thinking. Tracy seems to be highly impressed in this regard with the work of the French Catholic philosopher Jean-Luc Marion, *Dieu sans l'être* (Paris, 1982) — a highly suggestive two-track title: *God without being God*; *God without/other than being*. Tracy is primarily intrigued by Marion's elaboration of the thought of Dionysius the Areopagite and applauds Marion's brilliant retake on both excess and detachment in Pseudo-Dionysius (see "Literary Theory and Return of the Forms for Naming and Thinking God in Theology," 315). Marion offers a summary of his negative theology and a further analysis thereof in, "In the Name: How to Avoid Speaking of 'Negative Theology'," ed. J.D. Caputo & M.J. Scanlon, *God, the Gift and Postmodernism*, The Indiana Series in the Philosophy of Religion (Bloomington/Indianapolis, 1999) 20-41.

The hidden God

A second point of contact can be found in the *negative contrast experience* encountered in conflict and suffering and the *hiddenness of God* revealed therein. The God of the Christian narrative does not prevent conflict and suffering nor does God resolve it from without. God is not a factor of power or domination in the battleground of hegemonic narratives. In the context of human suffering and conflict, however, in the silence of those who have been robbed of the freedom to speak, God is revealed precisely in God's hiddenness. Such experience, moreover, teaches us to see that the very revelation of this hiddenness is the revelation of the reality of God.[10] God is part and parcel of human suffering, although not as its perpetrator. God takes the side of the sufferers and the victims.

Potential associations can also be drawn here with postmodern sensitivity: suffering is experienced as an 'event', as an aesthetic-ethical moment which brings about a rupture in the oppressive hegemonic narrative of the one who perceives suffering as suffering. Theologically speaking — i.e., within the contours of the Christian narrative — this irreducible aesthetic-ethical moment is judged to be the place in which the awareness of the hidden God is given concrete form. It is for this reason that the theology of the hidden God is, in the first instance, negative theology, *testimony to the 'non-presence' of God in suffering*. In an interview given on the occasion of his 80th birthday, Edward Schillebeeckx states: "For me God is only present as the absent God. His place is the moment of crisis, the dark night, the face of wounded

---

[10] This type of postmodern theology is qualified by Tracy as postmodern prophetical theology: this theology sees "the revelation of God's reality even as relational in the disclosure of God's weakness in the cross and God's conflict with the powers of this world a relational option for the oppressed of all history" (Tracy, "The Hermeneutics of Naming God," 263).

humanity."[11] Schillebeeckx maintains the possibility of discovering traces of God in one's personal engagement, in one's ethical commitment. "God can be made manifest in one's resistance to suffering not in suffering itself. Human persons transcend themselves in their salutary commitment to their fellow men and women. In such instances the requirements of justice take on excessive proportions, being transformed into selfless love and dedication."[12] When we act against suffering, God lays aside his hiddenness and comes close to us. Erik Borgman, a student of Schillebeeckx, offers a radical view of this perspective: "In my opinion, theology should make it clear in concrete — I would almost say: experiential — terms what it means to say that the Spirit of God hovered over the waters of chaos while the earth was formless and void and there was darkness over the face of the deep."[13] Borgman maintains the need for a theology that gives witness — in line with liberation theology — to the mystical insight "that the apparently powerless resistance [of the concrete poor, continually marginalized in their concrete and specific situation] which already accompanies the fact that suffering is experienced as suffering, is the mark of the hidden God of life."[14] It is precisely this experience that breaks through predominant and oppressive hegemonic narratives: the awareness of the hidden God made manifest in such experience drives one to immediate engagement, to witness, to ethical-political praxis.[15]

[11] J. Brok & J. Van Hooydonk, "'Voor mij is God alleen aanwezig als afwezige God'. Interview met E. Schillebeeckx," *De Bazuin* 77 (1994) 42, 4-7, p. 6.

[12] *Ibid.*

[13] E. Borgman, "Gods Geest over de wateren. Sporen van God temidden van de bedreigende moderniteit," *Tijdschrift voor de theologie* 32 (1992) 143-164, p. 158.

[14] *Ibid.*, p. 161. See further E. Borgman, *Alexamenos aanbidt zijn God. Theologische essays voor sceptische lezers* (Zoetermeer, 1994).

[15] See further L. Boeve, "Postmoderne politieke theologie? Johann Baptist Metz in een gesprek met het actuele kritische bewustzijn," *Tijdschrift voor theologie* 39 (1999) 244-264.

The absent God

Theologians detect a final point of contact between negative theology and postmodern sensitivity in the experience of the absent God, or rather the absence of the experience of God. God refuses to make Godself known, to be the subject of human experience. Indeed, there are no longer any signs that have the capacity to witness to God's presence. God is only present in God's *radical absence*. We will illustrate this position on the basis of the writings of Paul Moyaert and Denys Turner. Moyaert takes the actual absence of the experience of God in negative existential experience as his point of departure, while Turner builds upon the fundamental absence of the experience of the divine.

According to Moyaert[16], the theologian who would endeavour to practice negative theology today would be well advised not to focus too immediately on the *Deus semper major* and thereby fall into the trap of criticising every kind of discourse related to this ever-greater God. He suggests that theologians would do better to begin with negative existential experiences, which are, in essence, genuine experiences of transcendence (in the following sense: we experience the other and/or the world as such, as transcendent when the experience thereof encroaches upon my representations, expectations and desires etc., with respect to the world and the other). The experience of God that stands most in a class of its own is thus the experience of the *complete absence* of God, a negative existential experience that interrupts my own narrative (i.e., my immanent representations and desires). At the same time, however, that which "breaks through, interrupting this course, is not itself a

---

[16] P. Moyaert, "On Faith and the Experience of Transcendence: An Existential Reflection on Negative Theology," ed. I.N. Bulhof & L. ten Kate, *Flight of the Gods. Philosophical Perspectives on Negative Theology* (New York, 2000) 375-383.

course, is not itself a source of supplementary enrichment."[17] Such experiences of transcendence are not experiences of the fact that God's goodness is always greater and richer than our capacity to represent it. On the contrary, they consist precisely in the awareness that there are no signs in our world or in our lives (and memory) that by their very nature are capable of supporting our belief in God's goodness. "God's transcendence is manifest in the *suspension* of any sign of His goodness, which is to say in His radical absence. When every link between this world and God's goodness falls away, when that goodness is nowhere visible or when it is no longer mediated in any way, then faith can be nothing other than a suffering of God's transcendence. The faith that then sometimes perseveres is a faith that no longer has any sign to rely on. It is faith feeling its way in the darkness."[18]

Turner employs a quite different approach, rejecting in principle every so-called experience of God out of hand because the actual concept of experience we employ is *inadequate* and indeed incapable of explaining the classical mystical experience of God.[19] Based on his study of medieval apophatic/mystical theology, Turner criticises our modern (scientific) concept of experience that, when applied in theology, leads to theological positivism: by analogy with the (natural) sciences, mystical experience is supposed to serve as positive proof of the truth claims of religion. Thus mysticism is for theology what sensory experience is for the sciences. Such a vision, he maintains, does not do justice to mysticism and negative theology. According to Turner, the apophatic and the mystical do indeed belong to the method of theology, not as confirmation or

[17] *Ibid.*, 382-383.

[18] *Ibid.*, 383.

[19] See D. Turner, *The Darkness of God. Negativity in Christian Mysticism* (Cambridge, 1995).

proof but rather as a critical instance within the theological endeav-our. Mysticism does not offer proof, does not lead to 'discovery', rather it complicates, forces us to 'question' and to 'search'. As a matter of fact, negativity in classical mysticism is understood as the absence or negation of the experience of God and not the expe-rience of the negation or absence of God. God is not experienced; God, as present or absent, is not the object of human consciousness.

In this light, Turner rejects every 'mysticism' as the culture of determined experiences of inner depth, of perfect harmony. Mys-ticism is over-psychologised! In its original dynamic, however, it was intended to lead to anti-mysticism. Genuine mysticism, Turner argues, is to be found in the theological tradition that allows itself time and again to be disturbed and that makes such a *strategy of disturbance* a way of living. It should not come as much of a sur-prise, therefore, that Turner plainly insists that the very manner of thinking that we refer to as 'postmodern', that runs counter to the hegemonic master narratives, has the capacity to allow the contem-porary theologian to become aware once again of "the 'deconstruc-tive' potential of human thought and language which so character-ized classical mediaeval apophaticism."[20]

4. THE INCOMPREHENSIBLE, HIDDEN AND ABSENT GOD

The necessity as well as the consequences of an open Christian narrative would appear to have been confirmed once again by our reflections thus far. We have been able to establish that — via a resumption of the tradition of negative theology — a contemporary, *relevant and plausible (lack of) discourse and reflection on God* can be maintained on three distinct occasions. Such discourse and

---

[20] *Ibid.*, 8.

such reflection tend to avoid the pitfalls to which hegemonic narratives are prone while taking the theological critique thereof seriously. Instead of a God who functions in a narrative that enslaves and victimises people within its claim to conceptual supremacy, the Christian narrative revolutionises God from within to the extent that it is capable of opening itself towards God. This interruption in the Christian narrative takes place by preference where God as the Other manifests Godself in the concrete, oppressed other. By analogy with the conceptual patterns with which postmodern thinkers perceive reality (in their case, the reality of language), theologians today are able to attest to God's active involvement with the world and its inhabitants. From the theological perspective, the event that interrupts ongoing narratives — and can never be recuperated therein — reveals something of God.

This God of whom we speak is not at our disposal, not a God to be grasped and understood. Indeed, the God of whom we speak is not available for our comprehension and understanding. In the abundance and excess of love, God withdraws from every form of determination. This God is a God who appears to be absent in a world of suffering yet made manifest where rejection is observed and where oppression is resisted. This God is not a mere factor in our Christian narrative, nor a familiar element experienced as given within the boundaries of our (conceptual) universe, as burden of proof in function of our theological discourse on the truth. This God is only present in God's absence, as the boundary of every discourse.

Aside from the fact that every discourse about (the Christian) God outside the boundaries of the Christian narrative is as good as meaningless and that non-Christians will tend unavoidably to consider every attempt at recontextualising postmodern sensitivities in contemporary theology as mere recuperation, apophatic theology would appear nevertheless to have the potential to provide the Christian narrative today with contextual plausibility. It offers a point of departure from which the Christian narrative can be discussed at a time in which God would appear *de facto* to have little if any place, even for Christians. Apophatic theology, moreover, prevents the Christian narrative from becoming a narrative of certitude at a time in which all narratives are being put to the test. In our continuing but treacherous efforts to free ourselves of every from of existential uncertainty, apophatic theology helps us to avoid placing our trust in a 'safe' God as the ultimate guarantee of the truth of our narrative.

5. AN APOPHATIC THEOLOGY OF THE OPEN NARRATIVE?

A theology of the open narrative cannot avoid rooting itself in an *apophatic-theological attitude*. As an open narrative, the Christian narrative cultivates a contemplative openness that facilitates God's demanding interruption. This (grace) event cannot be exhaustively contained by Christian words, images, narratives, symbols and rituals, which are always particular, limited, contextually determined and fragmentary. While such determinations can never describe God, let alone attain him — they can only point to, or better still, testify to God — they remain our only means to refer to God, 'our means', 'our narrative'. Negative theology is not the last word on the matter. There can be no negative theology without positive theology, no pure 'openness' without 'narrative'. Negative theology forms, nevertheless, the critical, questioning background to every positive theological endeavour.[21]

---

[21] I have elaborated on these perspectives in "Postmodernism and Negative Theology. The A/theologie of the 'open narrative'," *Bijdragen. Tijdschrift voor filosofie en theology* 58 (1997) 407-425; and (with K. Feyaerts) in "Religious Metaphors in a Postmodern Culture. Transverse Links between Apophatical Theology and Cognitive Semantics," ed. Id., *Metaphor and God-talk*, Religions and Discourse, 2 (Canterbury, 1999) 153-184.

The past is replete with alternative ways to reflectively clarify God's involvement with his people. In a context in which belief in God is no longer evident as such, our awareness of God as the Other who always escapes us and 'is only present in God's absence' offers us a conceptual structure that helps us to come to terms with our actual condition. On the one hand, the fact that God does not have a 'place' in the Christian narrative and can only be evoked in God's incomprehensibility prevents us from falling foul once again of totalitarian claims.[22] On the other hand, however, contemporary Christians are also postmodern men and women, participants in a culture in which God's role is no longer evident and in which profound human or religious experiences no longer refer automatically to the God of Jesus Christ. Without the transmitted witness of God's involvement in the history of humanity and the world, and without communities that endeavour to make this witness contextually their own, God would remain inaccessible to us. Every context gives rise to new opportunities to recontextualise the Christian faith, in spite of the dangers such a process must involve. Our so-called postmodern context is no less such an opportunity.

Events can be discussed to death, rationalised away, especially when they are immediately interpreted from within one all-determining perspective. Perhaps, then, it is to our advantage that we are sometimes incapable of bringing God into the discussion as on the night of July 25th, 1996, and that we are sometimes forced to ask, 'Where were you, God?', as on August 22nd, 1996.

---

[22] This now religiously-motivated critical awareness prevents the contextual and theological accentuation of the option of faith as well as the particular character of the Christian narrative from being identified with traditionalistic reflexes. On the contrary, such accents imply a dynamic understanding of tradition that impels the Christian faith to engage in continual recontextualisation rooted in its sensitivity to interruption and held up against the praxis of the open narrative to which it provides concrete form.

IX. CHRISTIANITY INTERRUPTED
BY THE WORLD RELIGIONS

Perhaps more than ever before, Christians today are faced with a plurality of religions and other fundamental life-options. Typical of present day theology is the fact that such plurality has become a point of departure for theological reflection.[1] Religious diversity, and the religious authenticity experienced therein, has provided theologians with much food for thought, leading them to study the various world religions in order to understand them better. Contemporary theologians examine the relationship between Christianity and other world religions in an effort to establish a theology of non-Christian religions. They likewise study the potential for mutual agreement between the various world religions at the dogmatic and/or practical levels in order to establish an ecumenical theology, focusing in particular on the preconditions necessary for inter-religious dialogue that might provide the foundation for such mutual agreement. A variety of perspectives and standpoints concerning the possibility, importance, appropriateness, concrete form and expected results of such an undertaking have already been treated.[2]

However, at the same time, confrontation with other religions invites Christians to reflect on their own religion and its claims (universality, truth). Such reflection ought not to begin with questions concerning the identity of the other; or how the other is to be recognised by Christians; or how Christianity should distinguish

---

[1] See, for example, G. D'Costa, "The End of Systematic Theology," *Theology* 95 (1992) 324-334.

[2] For the impact of inter-religious dialogue on the field of ethics see, for example, H. Küng, *Project Weltethos* (Munich, 1990).

itself from other religions; or what Christianity and other religions can learn from one another; or how they should communicate and co-operate with one another. Christians are invited, rather, to situate themselves within the plural religious context. What does the situation of plurality say about the Christian narrative itself? In what way can the Christian narrative continue to hold its own in the midst of religious plurality? How can Christianity avoid the pitfalls of relativism?[3]

On the basis of two (three) comparisons, we will sketch the main features of a possible response to these questions: 'the parable of the men born blind and the elephant' ascribed to the Buddha — and a variation thereon — and 'the parable of the ring' from Lessing's 'Nathan the Wise'. Both parables frequently appear in discussions concerning the relationship between distinct (world) religions. Against the background of the postmodern context, and the irreducible plurality that resulted from the collapse of the master narratives, both parables offer contrasting perspectives on multiplicity and provide useful inspiration for a renewed characterisation of our own Christian narrative in light of the actual context.

1. THE MAN BORN BLIND AND THE ELEPHANT

The parable

Although this parable is often used to shed light on the relationship between the world religions, it actually stems from a different context.[4] Its starting point was not the context of religious plurality but rather a controversy between theological schools at the time of the Buddha. Representatives of the schools involved in the discussion,

---

[3] It should be clear that references will ultimately emerge in such a presentation of the question in response to the questions already summarised.

[4] For the account below, we have paraphrased the text provided in G. Mensching (ed.), *Buddhistische Geisteswelt. Vom Historischen Buddha zum Lamaismus*

ascetics and Brahmans, disputed one another's position, insisted on the veracity of their own particular claim to the truth and condemned each other's bogus assertions. They vehemently contested questions concerning the finality of the world, the essence of life or of the body and life after death.

Perplexed by this theological dispute, some monks sought advice from the Buddha who told them the following story. Once upon a time, the king of Savatthi brought together all the men born blind in his city in one place. He then brought forward an elephant and each of the blind men was invited to touch one part of its body while the king said, 'Now this is an elephant'. Some of the blind men felt the elephant's head, others an ear, and still others a tusk, the trunk, the torso, a leg, the hind quarters, the tail, the hairy tip of the tail, etc. Afterwards, the king asked the blind men what the elephant looked like. The ones who felt the head said that the elephant was like a huge cauldron. The ones who felt an ear said it was like a basket for sifting the grain; those who felt a tusk said a ploughshare; those who felt the trunk said the rod of a ploughshare; those who felt the torso said a grain silo; those who felt a leg said a pillar; those who felt the hind quarters said a cannon; those who felt the tail said a cudgel; those who felt the tip of the tail said a broom. Since the blind men were completely unable to agree among themselves about what an elephant actually looked like, they ended up in a fistfight, much to the consternation of the king. The Buddha then added to this story that the controversy between the theological schools was bound to end in the same way: because they are blind, the Brahmans and ascetics do not understand what the matter is all about; they cannot distinguish truth from untruth;

(Wiesbaden s.d.) 38-42 (for a broader discussion see, among others, G. Löhr, "Das Indische Gleichnis vom Elephanten und seine verschiedenen Deutungen. Zum Problem interreligiöser Toleranz und des interreligiösen Dialoges," *Zeitschrift für Missionswissenschaft und Religionswissenschaft* 79 (1995) 290-304).

they dispute with one another because they can only see one part and cannot view the whole.

Interpretations

Theologians who employ this parable to illustrate variety, division and struggle between the world religions[5] identify the latter with the blind men who turn to violence because their religious perspectives are mutually exclusive. A cauldron is clearly not a plough and a plough not a pillar. While the parable is thus able to represent religious struggle, evoking irreconcilable difference, it is also capable of offering a way out of the impasse. It offers insight into *the true essence* of religion that, for those who grasp it, provides a way to see through the contest apparently raging in religious plurality.

It is evident, of course, that the narrative of the man who felt the elephant's trunk sounds completely different from the narrative of the man who felt its leg or its tusk or its hind quarters or its tail. Each narrative, however, is equally true and equally faithful to reality. Moreover, the one who is able to listen to each narrative side by side or, better still, to overcome his or her blindness or, like the king, is not blind to start with, will ultimately realise that the actual narrative is about an elephant. All religions are true, albeit partially. They are *partial truths*, part of the complete narrative that is only clear to those who have sight. Religions are thus related to one another as parts of a universal religion — in the same way as the elephant's limbs are related to the elephant as a whole. An alternative interpretation of the parable maintains that, by analogy with the multiplicity that exists within Christianity itself, the various

---

[5] See, for example, J. Hick, *God and the Universe of Faiths. Essays in the Philosophy of Religion* (Houndsmills/Basingstoke/Hampshire/London, corr. ed. 1988) 140; G. D'Costa, "Toward a Trinitarian Theology of Religions," ed. C. Cornille & V. Neckebrouck, *A Universal Faith? Peoples, Cultures, Religions, and the Christ* (Fs. F. De Graeve) (Leuven, 1992) 139-154, pp. 143-144.

world religions are merely *confessions* of the same mono-religion. A similar interpretation holds that every religion is a *dogmatisation* of the same religious experience. The universal mono-religion that lies behind every particular religion is then understood to be purely mystical in character and un-dogmatic.

Can one maintain, therefore, that the sum of religious (Christian and non-Christian) narratives amounts to a religious meta-narrative? Is there one single narrative that speaks the language of God or can determine the divine will once and for all in its statements? The contrary would appear to be the case. The multiplicity of religious narratives evidently exhibit irreconcilable differences and do not tend to relate to one another as complementary fragments of the same 'reconstructable' original or as different versions of the same thing. Moreover: who is to determine the criteria whereby the various religions are to be reforged into one single religion? If one can agree to the existence of some mystical 'mono-religion', who is to provide the language necessary for the experience, mediation and community of faith that ultimately require a minimum of communicability?

Christianity according to the parable

In spite of the unanswered questions surrounding the interpretation of the parable, it nevertheless offers Christian theologians two specific ways in which to position the Christian narrative as such. In the first place, theologians might recognise themselves in the character of *the blind men*. This would then imply that they ought to try to rid themselves of their blindness and thus become aware of the fact that the Christian narrative only represents part of the truth. In their search for the fullness of truth, theologians have two options: they will either profoundly relativise the Christian narrative in function of a qualitatively superior mono-religion or endeavour to supplement elements from the Christian narrative with elements from other religious narratives in order to reconstruct the said mono-religion.

Both options fail to take the Christian narrative as a particular religion seriously. In addition, there is an evident lack of indication as to the nature of the mono-religion which is thus to be constructed, certainly in our postmodern context and the radical plurality that typifies it. What remains for the religious individual after such a *radical relativisation* of the world religions?

In the second instance, theologians are at liberty to identify themselves with *the king* in the parable rather than the blind men. While the king is clearly disconcerted by the blind men's aggression towards one another, this is probably due to the fact that he already knew (and saw) from the start that their dispute concerned an elephant. The king's confusion is that of a person who adopts a position of truth, the position of the mono-religion, and observes how this universal truth is torn apart and trampled upon by the other religions. The king also has two options: either he turns his back in disdain on the debacle and condemns the other religions as untrue, based on the criterion of his own Christian religion, which he considers to be universal (exclusivism), or he explains the (truth of the) other religions as part of his own all-embracing Christian religion (inclusivism). In contrast to the options resulting from identification with the men born blind, the Christian narrative clearly takes itself seriously — perhaps too seriously — in this instance and leaves virtually no space for other religions. Christianity thus imposes itself as a *universal meta-religion*.

A variation: the parable of the dew drop at sunrise

A popular variant of the parable of the blind men and the elephant is that of the dew drop at sunrise[6] that tells the story of a group of

---

[6] We use the version (with comments) in T. Andree, "Het interreligieuze leren," ed. H. Lombaerts & L. Boeve, *Traditie en initiatie. Perspectieven voor de toekomst*, Nikè-reeks, 36 (Leuven, 1996) 123-145, p. 132-133.

seven disciples who are enjoying a morning walk together with their master somewhere in the Far East. The dewdrops glisten in the early morning light. "Drawn to an exceptionally large dew drop, the master invited his disciples to stop and gather round it. He then asked his disciples what colour the dewdrop was. 'Red', said the first, 'orange', the second, 'yellow', the third, 'green', the fourth, 'blue', the fifth, 'purple', the sixth and 'violet', the seventh. Surprised by these differences and each of them certain that they had had a clear view of the dewdrop, the disciples almost came to blows. The master then told them to change places with one another. Slowly but surely they began to realise that, in spite of their different observations, each of them had spoken the truth."

In the version of the parable we have followed here, the interpretation thereof follows immediately upon the event itself. The parable goes on to relate how the master further enlightens his disciples: truth, he tells them, is like the dewdrop; the way we see it depends on our perspective. He continues: "You need to acquire every truth because together they form the true light, the fullness of the truth. Until you have become one of the Great Ones and are able to observe the seven colours all at once, you will observe the truth in a different way and adopt a different perspective with every reincarnation. You should not only be tolerant, therefore, [...] but you should be happy that there are other opinions. For as long as you yourself are unable to see the light in its fullness you will need your fellow disciples to help you comprehend the whole truth."

Once again Christian theologians would appear to have two options in their efforts to clarify the position of the Christian faith in light of the parable — analogous to the possibilities offered by the parable of the blind men and the elephant. The Christian faith can adopt the position of one of the *disciples* and face profound *relativisation* as one perspective among several others that only together constitute the fullness of the truth. Here too the result is a mono-religion that, beyond all other religions, is capable of unifying and sublimating the different colour perspectives in the full light of the whole truth. The theologian is also at liberty to consider the Christian narrative to be that of the *master* who has already seen the light in all its fullness. Once again this can lead to an *exclusivistic* option (all other religions are inferior) or an *inclusivistic* option (the fragmentary truth of the other religions is already included in the Christian truth). What remains, however, is the invitation to the other 'to become one of the Great Ones and thus observe all seven colours at once': only by becoming Christian is it possible to see the light in its fullness.

The parables in light of contemporary critical consciousness

The question remains, however, as to the theologian's capacity to actually follow these two avenues: one that would obliterate Christianity as a religious narrative and another that would lead to the absolutisation of Christianity as the only narrative, a hegemonic, totally embracing, religious meta-narrative. In our postmodern context, the latter option would be particularly problematic. For a religion that hopes to recontextualise itself as an open narrative, such a trap ought to be avoided at all costs — in spite of the fact that the apparent increase in religious fundamentalism would seem to illustrate the contrary. The option to obliterate one's own religious narrative likewise offers little in the way of future perspective. Not only does it fail to provide an alternative religious meta-narrative, it also assumes that the end of the master narratives must imply the end of every narrative, in this case the Christian narrative. Postmodern men and women are also in need of orientation and integration — albeit no longer in the form of all-embracing and hegemonic meta-narratives whether religious in character or not. In what follows we will attempt to show how an open Christian narrative can productively position itself in our plural context on the basis of a third comparison, the parable of the ring.

2. THE PARABLE OF THE RING

The parable of the ring, taken from the play 'Nathan the Wise' written in 1779 by Gotthold Ephraim Lessing (1729-1781), offers a different perspective on the relationship between the diverse religious narratives to that of the parable of the elephant.[7] A brief sketch of the parable will help to illustrate what we mean.

The parable

Sultan Saladin asked Nathan, a wise Jew, to tell him which religion, Judaism, Christianity or Islam, possessed the fullness of the truth. In reply to this question, Nathan told the following parable. A man had a ring of priceless value that also possessed the mysterious power to make the one who wore it on his finger beloved before God and his fellow human beings. It is hardly surprising, Nathan continued, that this man always wore the ring and desired to keep it in his family after his death. With this in mind, therefore, he determined that the bearer of the ring had to pass it on to his most beloved son who would then immediately become the head of the family. And so it happened: the ring was passed on from father to son and thus from generation to generation. There came a time, however, when a man had three sons whom he loved equally and he simply could not decide which son to choose and which two to disappoint. He decided, therefore, to have a jeweller make two other rings identical to the original ring. He gave each son his blessing and a ring and passed away. The sons came together and wanted to ascertain which one of them had the father's original ring and should thus take his place as head of the family. Given that the three rings were identical, however, they were

---

[7] See G.E. Lessing, *Werke*, ed. H.G. Göpfert (Munich, 1971) vol. 2, 205-343, pp. 275-280.

unable to come to a decision. Of course, each of the sons considered himself to be the bearer of the original ring and each was determined to become the head of the family: after all, the father could not have deceived his most beloved son. The implication was likewise clear that each son considered his two brothers to be engaged in some treacherous game. Fraternal conflict inevitably ensued and they decided to settle the matter by calling upon the services of a judge. Each in turn swore before the judge that he had received the genuine ring from his father.

So much for the first part of the parable. As in the parable of the elephant, plurality and diversity in the parable of the ring end up in conflict. In an insightful and intriguing manner, Nathan (Lessing) is able to reveal the nature of the conflict that arises when one religion pretends to possess the whole truth. Not only does the one son feel short-changed when the other two claim to be in possession of the truth themselves, he also suspects them of wilful foul play. After all, the father could only give but one ring; and yet each son is convinced that his father gave it to him. The judge is faced with a difficult task. In contrast to the king, who clearly saw the elephant and became disconcerted and displeased with the futile brawl between the blind men, the judge sees but three perfectly similar rings. There is no law to help him decide and no criterion on which he can base his judgement. Or is there! We return to the parable.

The judge's ultimate decision is unexpected: considering the fact that the real ring was said to make its bearer acceptable before God and his fellow human beings, and considering that the three brothers clearly did not love one another or consider themselves beloved of one another, all three rings must evidently be false. The real ring must have gone missing. In spite of this logic, however, the judge does not consider it wise to simply throw the rings away. He thus offers the sons the following advice: "Each of you received a ring from your father and each of you is certain that he possesses the original ring":

"It is possible that your father
could no longer bear the tyranny of having one ring in his household.
It is beyond doubt that he loved all three of you,
and loved you equally:
indeed, the last thing he wanted was to brush two of you aside
and favour only one. Very well then!
Let each of you strive after a love
which is unbiased and free from prejudice.
Let each of you strive with one another
to manifest the power in the stone of his ring.
Come to the aid of this power with gentleness,
with heartfelt tolerance, with generosity
and with the most fervent submission to God.
When the powers of the stone manifest themselves
among your great grandchildren,
then I invite you after a thousand thousand years
to come before this judgement seat once again.
A wiser man than I shall be sitting in judgement.
Go now, concluded the modest judge."[8]

As far as the judge is concerned the matter is clear. He has no grounds on which to determine the genuineness of the rings. If the original ring had been lost it was perhaps for the best, considering the father could not choose which of his three sons to favour above the others. The genuine ring, which spelled tyranny for his entire household,

---

[8] "Möglich; daß der Vater nun / Die Tyrannei des Einen Rings nicht länger / In seinem Hause dulden wollen! — Und gewiß; / Daß er euch alle drei geliebt, und gleich / Geliebt: indem er zwei nicht drücken mögen, / Um einen zu begünstigen. — Wohlan! / Es eifre jeder seiner unbestochnen / Von Vorurteilen freien Liebe nach! / Es strebe von euch jeder um die Wette, / Die Kraft des Steins in seinem Ring' an Tag / Zu legen! komme dieser Kraft mit Sanftmut, / Mit herzlicher Verträglichkeit, mit Wohltun, / Mit innigster Ergebenheit in Gott, / Zu Hülf'! Und wenn sich dann der Steine Kräfte / Bei euern Kindes-Kindeskindern äußern: / So lad' ich über tausend tausend Jahre, / Sie wiederum vor diesen Stuhl. Da wird / Ein weisrer Mann aus diesem Stuhle sitzen, / Als ich; und sprechen. Geht! — So sagte der / Bescheidne Richter" (*Ibid.*, 280).

was lost forever. What remained were the three rings that, although not original, still served as a reminder of the lost ring and the power in which they shared. The one who testifies in his life and deeds to this power ('comes to its aid') shall experience it for himself.

Interpretations

Many interpretations of this parable tend to foist a complete religious relativism on Lessing; others are of the opinion that he reduces religion to ethical praxis, to a kind of religion of humanity.[9] Such interpretations, however, do not do justice to the author of our parable. His primary aim was to show that a religion's claim to universal truth and validity cannot be coercively legitimised. For Lessing this was more a question of the specific nature of *religious truth* rather than the rejection of religion as such. Far from being an independent datum, religious truth, according to Lessing, is woven into the fabric of our 'most profound submission to God' ('Mit innigster Ergebenheit in Gott'). Religious truth is a deeply-rooted element of our affection for God, of our complete abandonment to God. Religious truth functions within the relationship of trust we enjoy with God. In this perspective, it cannot simply be maintained that Lessing reduces religion to ethics: even ethical praxis acknowledges its roots in this relationship. Lessing, rather, is in search of the core of religion that ultimately cannot be objectivised or grasped.

---

[9] For this paragraph, see A. Schilson, "'Nathan der Weise' als poetische Predigt über die wahre Religion," *Theologie und Glaube* 85 (1995), 518-532, p. 522ff; see also: Id., "Zur Wirkungsgeschichte Lessings in der katholischen Theologie," ed. H. G. Göpfert, *Das Bild Lessings in der Geschichte* (Heidelberg, 1981) 69-92. For a similar, but more pronounced interpretation, see H. Küng, "Religion im Prozeß der Aufklärung," W. Jens & H. Küng, *Dichtung und Religion* (Munich, 1985) 82-101.

Christianity and the world religions

What then does our parable teach us about the relationship between the various religions and, more specifically, about the Christian narrative? Religions, including the Christian religion, are like the rings. They refer to a primordial narrative that ultimately cannot be narrated (is lost?). As distinct religious narratives (traditions) they constitute particular yet irreducible ways of referring to, representing and bearing witness to the inexpressibility of the Truth. This truth is not an object of knowledge, to be mastered, grasped exhaustively in language. One can only have access to it in a relational manner, encounter it in faith as grace.

In the postmodern context, Christianity as a master narrative has also lost much of its credibility — in spite of the fact that many see the fall of the modern master narratives as an opportunity for narrating a new Christian master narrative. Christianity, however, has no future as an all-encompassing meta-narrative, but only as a small narrative, or better still as an open narrative, as a narrative that offers orientation and integration without thereby being determined to integrate everything into its own narrative in a totalitarian way.[10] In our current situation, the Christian narrative relativises itself because it acknowledges the *Deus semper major*, not because there are other narratives that might be equally true and that might constitute a single piece of some greater, 'real', primordial narrative (the elephant). One's own tradition, one's own images and concepts — all of which have developed from concrete, historically-situated contexts — ought to be expressions of that openness. When the narrative closes itself and determines to enclose God, openness disappears and God withdraws.

As an open narrative, therefore, the Christian narrative relativises itself, by bearing witness to the ever-greater God. At the same time,

[10] See Part 2.

however, it takes itself very seriously: it is only in particular narratives, concrete images and contextual thought patterns that it can bear witness to human submission to, relationship with and affection towards God. Grounded in this insight into its own (irreducibly) particular character as reference, the Christian narrative exercises modesty towards other religious narratives — at least towards 'open' forms of such narratives — and abandons its pretensions to absoluteness while continuing to take itself seriously. It continues to perceive itself as a language that enjoys access to the inexpressible as reference. It continues to take itself seriously because, as a narrative, it constitutes a specific, always particular, context-determined and, in the light of this context, irreplaceable witness to that which transcends its witnessing. Even though it is confronted with a plurality of such narratives (or indeed precisely because of the confrontation), it is aware, nonetheless, of its *irreducible intrinsic value*. It is aware that a Christian open narrative, as a historically and contextually-rooted witness to the ungraspable and unexpected yet hoped for grace, opens a way towards God and for God.

Where the Christian narrative is able to acquire this awareness and present itself as an open narrative, it will not only liken itself to one of the rings in the parable, but also (and at the same time) to the 'modest judge'. While the latter rebukes those narratives that tend to close themselves up in a dominating way, he likewise defers judgement.[11] The same is true of Saladin who, after hearing the parable of Nathan the wise, no longer wanted to judge whether Judaism, Christianity or Islam had the ultimate hold on the truth. Final judgement is deferred — until God comes.

---

[11] Observe, for that matter, the striking parallel between the manner of Nathan's judge and the role and bearing of the figure of the judge in the argument of Jean-François Lyotard as an image for the discourse of the philosopher (*Le différend* (Paris, 1983); *L'enthousiasme. La critique kantienne de l'histoire* (Paris, 1986)).

3. NOTE ON THE RELATIVE IMPORTANCE OF THE CHRISTIAN TRADITION

Now that we have brought to an end our endeavour to recontextualise, and bearing in mind the actions of the judge in Lessing's parable, we conclude this third part of our study with a brief note on the Christian concept of tradition. Our postmodern context also exhibits evidence of the double temptation to traditionalism and the hunger for adaptation. In both instances, the dynamic surrounding the relationship between the inheritor of the tradition and the one passing it on is interrupted. The tradition is seen as either a survival from the past or as a superseded past — not as a living and life giving memory in the present and for the future, living tradition as the fruit of interaction between transmitted memory and actual context.

Those who consider themselves part of the Christian tradition, which they adjudge to be a contextual testimony to the original, in itself inexpressible Tradition,[12] will tend to be aware of *the relative importance of tradition*. We will support this claim with three arguments, which together constitute a theological legitimisation of the recontextualising perspective we have endeavoured to maintain.

In the first place, tradition deserves to be taken seriously because it offers us (Christians) unique access to the Tradition, making it possible to engage it in human discourse. The Christian tradition is of extreme importance because it constitutes *our own narrative about God and humanity*.

At the same time, however, the importance of the tradition we have inherited should not be absolutised. We speak of the *relative* importance of the tradition because it constitutes *our* narrative about *God* and *humanity*. It relates to our unique endeavour — necessarily particular and contextual — to express the Inexpressible.

---

[12] The first 'dogmatic-theological' meaning of Tradition refers to the original event of 'God's self-revelation'. See also chapter 1.

Given the necessarily historical, particular and contextual character of the relationship between tradition and Tradition, the former can only survive (and thus the latter also?) when it *continues to be our narrative about God and humanity*. The ancient words, stories and deeds that we have inherited require ongoing recontextualisation as the context in which we find ourselves changes. Our inheritance thus re-acquires its place in our actual Christian narrative. Only then can the living tradition we inherit be passed on to others and new Christians be integrated into the narrative.

In other words, as Christians we have received (what we refer to as) the self-manifestation of the divine via the Christian tradition, the narrative in which we are initiated. As Christians, we employ the historically-transmitted words of this narrative to speak of the surplus value of human existence (to which we have access via these words). We can only succeed in this endeavour, however, to the extent that the said words, in an ongoing historical-contextual process of recontextualisation, are attuned to this surplus value and can evoke the latter in such a way that it can become experience.

If the tradition understands itself as the transmitted word that testifies to the inexpressible divine Word, it will be impossible to reduce Christianity to a closed hegemonic narrative. To the extent that the Christian narrative is able to recognise alternative and authentic forms of bearing witness to the Inexpressible in other narratives — in spite of the fact that full access to such narratives remains difficult and one may encounter irreconcilability — it will likewise be able to recognise its own relativity. At the same time, however, for those of us who consider ourselves part of the Christian narrative, this same narrative is the *only* way in which we can express the Inexpressible.

EPILOGUE

Having drawn the process of recontextualisation, which has been the primary subject of our study, to a (provisional) close, we will conclude with a reflection on the position of the Christian in the contemporary world, summarised in six accents.

Faith as choice... Where membership of a particular religious group is no longer supported by one's social and cultural context and affiliations, faith as faith takes on its own specific profile. Christianity has made the transition from being a cultural religion to being a religion of faith. The Church no longer enjoys a monopoly position into which one is simply born but has become a Church of volunteers. In this new context, faith is not only a socio-structural option, it is a genuine 'faith option': the explicit choice for the Christian narrative as the interpretative framework of our thoughts, words and deeds and thus the specific option for God who has revealed Godself in history as love, *par excellence*, in Jesus of Nazareth, God's interrupter. In this perspective, conversion, discipleship and Church formation naturally enjoy a somewhat sharper focus.

... for a particular narrative. The uncertainty of our context also continues to have its effect on Christians, even when they are still inclined to entrust themselves to the dynamics of what is revealed in the Christian tradition. Indeed, the Christian faith, as has often been accepted in the past, lacks any absolute and demonstrable philosophical or ontological foundation in reality upon which it can ground, confirm and rationally elaborate its claims ('thinking' corresponds to 'being'): faith remains faith, a desire to enter into the narrative, and implies an ongoing search for God and God's salvific will for human persons and the world.

Such a 'faith option' likewise and immediately implies a *religiously-motivated critical consciousness*. For the believer, God and God's salvific action will constitute the 'o/Other' in the fullest sense of the word. This 'o/Other' cannot be appropriated to our own advantage. It continues to elude us, to evade our attempts to take hold of it and understand it for ourselves. No more idols, no more sacrifices, no more *Gott-mit-uns*, but rather a God who becomes visible in the poor, in the marginalized and the oppressed, in those who desire to share the vulnerability of the vulnerable. For Christians in the present context, sensitivity towards the 'threatened other' and resistance towards the 'threatening other' is ultimately a theologically-motivated task. The intensity and authenticity of the Christian lifestyle can only benefit from this. It goes without saying that this critical consciousness, in line with Jesus' condemnation of the Pharisees, will also at times have to be turned against certain forms of Christian religion when it becomes clear that the latter are no longer able to exercise it.

Those who genuinely desire to familiarise themselves with the Christian narrative, however, will ultimately have to develop a taste for it. Only those who enter into discipleship can come to learn what it means to believe that God is love, that we have been given the gift of grace in Jesus, and so forth. Christianity cannot be explained and communicated to the last detail and cannot be made completely transparent. Indeed, where efforts were made to do so in modern times, Christianity tended to be rather abruptly reduced to ethics and the upholding of values. While the same can perhaps be said for every other fundamental life-option, the very theological foundations of the Christian faith serve to intensify matters where Christianity is concerned. As a matter of fact, it would seem appropriate for Christians in the public forum, that the *arcanum* (Lat. 'secret', 'about which one remains silent') be reintroduced, in line with the early Church, and precisely out of respect for their deepest motivation. In a life of faith, which has its theological explanation in the relationship between God and humankind, there remain dimensions that cannot be communicated to those who do not share this faith, dimensions that have their roots in the said relationship.

No functional reduction. The cultural-philosophical and socio-logically oriented analysis of certain textual units in the present study might have left the reader with the impression that the Christian faith can only be considered relevant in the postmodern context as a meaning-giving framework and pattern of integration. It has to be made clear, however, that for Christians, faith and tradition can never be reduced to such socio-cultural functionality. Individualised as they may be, postmodern Christians are not Christians because they desire to play an active role in the construction of their own iden-tity or give meaning to their existence or introduce structure into the chaos of plurality in a critical and responsible manner. Christians are Christians because they consider themselves summoned to be so by the God made manifest in Jesus Christ. They do not honour their tradition because it facilitates the construction of a stable identity or provides meaning. They do so, rather, because their tradition speaks of a God who fascinates them and summons them to conversion and discipleship. It is in this sense that many Christians, in spite of their awareness that faith is one option among many at the socio-structural level, continue to experience this option as a vocation.

Rooted in their experience of the richness of their faith, Chris-tians will also continue to consider themselves called to pass on their faith within the context of one or other form of *missionary engagement*, precisely because their incorporation in the dynamic of the faith relationship and the faith community provides them with a sense of fulfilment. When a believer speaks from experi-ence and with respect for the *arcanum* over his or her faith, such words will always exhibit something of the character of witness in the actual context in which they are spoken. While those who subscribe to a different fundamental life option may not agree with what they hear, the authenticity thereof may well have the potential to leave a lasting impression.

***

After seven years of drudgery in a foreign land and before heading for home, Hans received a lump of gold as big as his head for his wages. Along the way, he met a knight and because he found the lump of gold too heavy, he exchanged it for the knight's horse. Still unsatisfied, however, he later exchanged the horse for a cow, the cow for a pig, the pig for a fat goose, and finally the goose for a grindstone and a white pebble. When Hans, fatigued by the journey, stooped over a well to drink, both stones fell into the well. Content that he was also relieved of these burdens, he continued his journey with a light heart. Freed from all his cares and worries he arrived home.[1]

Has the Christian faith not fared likewise? Were the numerous re-appropriations of the content of faith, under the pressures of modernity, not ongoing processes of relativisation; so much so that in the end, instead of valuable gold, what remained was a worthless pebble that could easily be missed? Are we not now living with the painful awareness that a great deal of valuable tradition has been lost — just as Hans' apparent contentment will be altered into discontent once he discovers what he has squandered away?[2]

---

[1] Based on one of the fairy tales of the Brothers Grimm entitled *Happy Hans*.

[2] The fairy tale, 'Happy Hans', by the Brothers Grimm was used in 1968 by Joseph Ratzinger, curial cardinal since 1981 and prefect of the Congregation for the Doctrine of the Faith in the Vatican, to illustrate the pernicious consequences of the increasing adaptation of the Christian faith to the modern world. He concluded the fairy tale: "How long Hans remained in this state of mistiness, how dark it was at the moment he was awakened from the dream of his supposed freedom, this is what the story [...] leaves to the fantasy of the reader." (*Einführung*

But perhaps Happy Hans did not become quite so unhappy as one might well have expected of someone who had consciously squandered a large amount of gold. In the course of a long journey, a massive piece of gold is ultimately a heavy burden, however valuable it may seem. Understood as a unified mass of content, tradition can be more of a burden for Christians than a blessing — the Christian's journey is, after all, never finished. An open concept of tradition, however, does not lend itself to comparison with an inert lump of gold. Perhaps such an open concept should be compared with a compass that, wherever one may be in the world, always points north and thus helps one in finding the right direction to follow.[3]

---

in das Christentum. Vorlesungen über das Apostolische Glaubensbekenntnis (Munich, 1968) 9.)

[3] Cf. L. Boeve, "Between Relativizing and Dogmatizing. A Plea for an Open Concept of Tradition," *East Asian Pastoral Review* 32 (1995) 327-340.

PRINTED ON PERMANENT PAPER • IMPRIME SUR PAPIER PERMANENT • GEDRUKT OP DUURZAAM PAPIER - ISO 9706

N.V. PEETERS S.A., WAROTSTRAAT 50, B-3020 HERENT